D1740139

Design,
technology,
empathy.

A contemporary issue in the conception and production of artifacts

First published in 2019
as part of the Design Principles and Practices Book Imprint
http://doi.org/10.18848/978-1-86335-160-7/CGP (Full Book)

Common Ground Research Networks
2001 South First Street, Suite 202
University of Illinois Research Park
Champaign, IL
61820

Library of Congress Cataloging-in-Publication Data

Names: Paris, Spartaco, 1973- author.
Title: Design, technology, empathy : a contemporary issue in the conception
  and production of artifacts / Spartaco Paris.
Description: Champaign : Common Ground Research Networks, 2019. | "This book collects in a
  revised form a series of short essays written and published by the author between 2013 and 2017,
  as the editor of the Rassegna Section in Domus"--Preface. | Includes bibliographical references. |
Summary: "Just as was the case in other phases of history - including, but not limited to pre-modern
  history - today's finishes in architecture and in our habitat are characterised by figures and spaces,
  rather than forms, increasingly moving away from abstraction. The recurrent and once again
  customary presence of figures, natural references, small or large-sized ornaments and decorations,
  calls for a reflection on this phenomenology; this ranges from a detail in texture to the finishing
  elements in our interiors, to the surfaces which attribute expressive features to contemporary
  buildings, in a sort of new - unconscious?- reference to a materialist and naturalistic matrix in
  relation to the look of artifacts. This condition seemed prevalent from, for example, a walk through
  the grounds at the last Expo: a touch of experimentalism in the expressive display of shapes and
  figures inspired by nature or biophysics. This is an easy tool to 'shock the bourgeoisie': from trees
  of life, foliage and/or stylized woods covering pavilions/boxes, to simplified naturalistic intrusions,
  the character of the array of decor for our habitat - from public spaces to homes - investigates a
  wide range of figures mimicking nature. The texts are organised into homogeneous thematic
  clusters, collecting reflections and short essays, with some bibliographic annotations for each topic.
  The central thread connecting the text is a critical approach - in positive terms - to the relation
  between technology, design concept and the production of forms of artifacts"-- Provided by
  publisher.
Identifiers: LCCN 2019024192 (print) | LCCN 2019024193 (ebook) | ISBN 9781863351584
  (hardback) | ISBN 9781863351591 (paperback) | ISBN 9781863351607 (pdf)
Subjects: LCSH: Design--Philosophy. | Interior decoration. | Architecture--Details. | Product design--
  Psychological aspects. | Empathy in art.
Classification: LCC NK1505 .P36 2019 (print) | LCC NK1505 (ebook) | DDC 747--dc23
LC record available at https://lccn.loc.gov/2019024192
LC ebook record available at https://lccn.loc.gov/2019024193

Cover: graphic processing of pattern from "Detail of iron cast element of facade, No.11 Albemarle Street,
  Paul Smith London flagship, designers: 6a architects, London, 2013" @courtesy of 6a architects

Design, technology, empathy.

A contemporary issue in the conception and production of artifacts

Spartaco Paris

COMMON
GROUND

DESIGN PRINCIPLES
AND PRACTICES

PREFACE

This book collects in a revised form a series of short essays written and published by the author between 2013 and 2017, as the editor of the *Rassegna Section* in *Domus*.

Contents are organized into homogeneous thematic clusters, ranging from design to technology, concept and production.

Nowadays, design language and finishes are redefined through images and spaces that appear to move increasingly away from abstraction.

In the 1970s, Manfredo Tafuri's renowned essay entitled *Architecture and Utopia* made an important contribution to defining - in a sort of manifesto - the role of design within society. Nowadays, at a time when it is increasingly difficult to define shared needs and scenarios towards projects for the common good, a new dyad, 'Design and Empathy', seems to be a good summary of the expanding range of individual needs and desires the design promises to satisfy.

The recurring presence of a new figurative representation of the expressive quality of artifacts - buildings and objects alike, both material and immaterial - is symptomatic of a search for a more user-friendly understanding. As a matter of fact, the fast pace imposed on life today requires the use of high-impact formal solutions, where immediate 'aesthetic appeal' is disconnected from long or pondered contemplation. This is why the 'abstract'- as opposed to the empathic - approach has been given less space and has been confined to minimalist interventions, or to cases where the intention is to give a tactile and perceptive characterisation to surface materials, using designs based on transparency, reflection and sheen.

There is much evidence of this phenomenon to be seen wandering around any architecture, design or art trade fair or exhibition. In order to better understand the contours of this phenomenon, it is useful to make reference to the concept of empathy as defined by Wilhelm Worringer's theories on the psychology of style (which marketing strategies currently applied to products for our living space unconsciously seem to make reference to).

The whole world of the image, notably that of digital animation, tends to offer hyper-realistic aesthetic simulacra based on expanded mimesis and altered nature: this is the world of visual stimuli in which we are immersed daily, a far cry from the abstract modernity that we used to face in the last millennium.

This is why we are witnessing the extension of an infinite landscape - which harks back to images from the Arts and Crafts movement - of finishes and surfaces, which may be reproduced today with the use of endless digital algorithms and which explicitly renew the figurative repertoire, reinstating the urge to mimic nature.

This clearly marks a return, with updated tools, to the field of applied arts, where a new virtuosity - technology - regains a bizarre value. What seems to have recently prevailed is the idolizing of the technical dimension of know-how (*können*) over artistic intention (*wollen*).

This condition can affect educational approaches to design, requiring a new way of thinking technology, methods and tools for the training and teaching of design: a new attitude towards the materiality of things, alongside the evanescent, immaterial illusion of the Internet of things.

Domus magazine has always devoted a special section of its contents, called 'Rassegna', to a reasoned and annotated selection of materials and products for the human habitat. The products presented are mainly the result of research and innovation on the part of cutting-edge or emerging companies operating within the multi-faceted areas of living space - from product design, to furniture, finishes and construction components and systems. Until the coming of the Internet and the development of digital products portals, *Domus' Rassegna* was - for a community of professionals, students and scholars - a reference 'construction archive', selected through the cultural filter of the Editorial Board and the series of Chief Editors that have been at the head of the magazine. The magazine authoritativeness has always been in itself an informal way of making a selection, on the part of those companies that had all the interest in being represented by their best production. With the spread of on-line product-archives, capable of updating in real time the constant multiplication of products, the role of the *Rassegna* in the printed version of *Domus* magazine has required a revision and new developments.

A special section of the magazine web portal is devoted to product communication and information, referring back to the *Rassegna* section in the printed version for a more thorough analysis of the topics covered each time, thus being more than a mere 'news' section. Reflection is therefore addressed not only on the formal outcome of products, but also on industrial production and the development of new technology.

From the first magazine subtitle, *Architettura e arredamento dell'abitazione moderna in città e in campagna* (*Architecture and Décor of the Modern Home in the City and in the Country*) to *Domus. Arte della casa* (*Domus. The Art of the Home*) and *I Quaderni* in the 1940s and 1950s, to the sections on how to 'Set up a home', the magazine has always focused its attention and research on seemingly 'minor', yet essential topics for our habitat.

The titles of the eleven instalments of *I Quaderni di Domus* provide evidence of this sensitivity towards functions and elements during the transformation of the Italian home against the backdrop of the modernisation process in our country. For example, the instalment *La Cucina* (The Kitchen), edited by Marco Zanuso, covers a basic, practical topic - yet an extremely modern and innovative one for a country under reconstruction; or green spaces, which were an opportunity for Luigi Figini to conduct a study, resulting in a specific Notebook; displays and elements for decoration and representation of the home 'modern' decor, such as *Tende* (Curtains), are the subject covered in the instalment by Cini Boeri[4]. The relation between the innovation of (artisanal and industrial) production and the opportunities for the formal and aesthetic transformation of living space and the quality of home life has been at the core of the magazine's innovative function.

And so, today, the *Rassegna* covers - cyclically, but not taxonomically - the products and components of contemporary living space: Kitchen, Bathroom, Furniture, Doors and Windows, Office, Lighting, Facades, Finishes, Technical Lighting, Outdoors.

The opening editorial, which I wrote starting from Nicola di Battista's arrival as editor-in-chief of the magazine in 2013, has the specific intention of reflecting precisely on the relations between the evolution of technology and the production of materials and their implications, both formal and in terms of product language. The following texts are a collection of the opening editorials, from November 2013 to July 2017. The collection is representative of a wide range of topics covered, in line with the thematic programme defined each year with the Chief Editor and the Editorial Board. This activity, which entails a cyclical reiteration of the topics covered, undoubtedly makes it possible to offer a progressively closer examination of the subjects under discussion. While reading the short collection of texts that follow, it is possible to highlight some common, cross-cutting considerations in the diverse topics covered.

As the *Rassegna* is mainly centred around components having a decorative or representative function, it has been possible to notice the supremacy of the representative function of the contemporary habitat over other roles of architecture.

Indeed, Loos himself claimed that a true architect always thinks in terms of skin, of surface, because surface affects the reactions of those inhabiting it. Through a meaningful sample of products investigated over 4 years of contributions, it is useful to underline a consideration in relation to the form and, at the same time, the production, which characterises and brings together the multiple array of products in today's habitat, in spite of existing differences. Just as was the case in other phases of history - including, but not limited to pre-modern history - today's finishes in architecture and in our habitat are characterised by figures and spaces, rather than forms, increasingly moving away from abstraction. The recurrent and once again customary presence of figures, natural references, small or large-sized ornaments and decorations, calls for a reflection on this phenomenology; this ranges from a detail in texture to the finishing elements in our interiors, to the surfaces which attribute expressive features to contemporary buildings, in a sort of new - unconscious?- reference to a materialist and naturalistic matrix in relation to the look of artifacts. This condition seemed prevalent from, for example, a walk through the grounds at the last Expo: a touch of experimentalism in the expressive display of shapes and figures inspired by nature or biophysics. This is an easy tool to 'shock the bourgeoisie': from trees of life, foliage and/or stylized woods covering pavilions/boxes, to simplified naturalistic intrusions, the character of the array of decor for our habitat - from public spaces to homes - investigates a wide range of figures mimicking nature.

The texts are organised into homogeneous thematic clusters, collecting reflections and short essays, with some bibliographic annotations for each topic. The central thread connecting the text is a critical approach - in positive terms - to the relation between technology, design concept and the production of forms of artifacts.

INTRODUCTION

Periodically, some terms or words - first moving through specific contexts and registers and then ending up in the common language - help represent the spirit of their time. Recently, the term 'empathy' has shown up repeatedly in different contexts: from politics - as a noble 'surrogate' of 'gut reasoning', in opposition to 'rational reasoning' - to sociology, marketing and design. This text aims at investigating a phenomenon that is strictly linked to this word, which has overtly been characterising the formal outcomes in the field of artifact design and - in its diverse scales and sizes - has become common ground from architecture to design, confirming the supremacy of the empathic component between individuals and artifacts. This condition of interaction has attributed a new role and semantic value to the surface of things, becoming a field of design investigation on the renewal of classic formal topics: decoration, representation, materiality. Chronologically placing this gradual supremacy of surface empathy in an accurate manner is all but simple. Yet, there is no doubt that, starting from the 2000s, several facts - associated to new technology (IIT) as well as to social change - have contributed to transforming the relationships between people and materiality, with a preference for those based on the *sense-feel-think-act-relate*[1] categories, with objects and devices alike, in a sort of new, consolatory materialism. This essay does not intend to investigate the reasons underlying such a phenomenon, which characterises the whole range of aesthetic expression, from cinema to arts, from architecture to design. As early as 2002, in her *Atlas of Emotion: Journeys in Art, Architecture and Film* - an essay that has become a world reference, across different aesthetic disciplines (cinema, architecture, arts) - Giuliana Bruno (Bruno, 2002) investigated the emotional dynamics at work in the interaction between the individual and artistic expression, through the movement and the universe of feelings; more recently, by considering the two-dimensional surface of things not only as a medium, but also as a new field of meanings[2] (Bruno, 2014). The several perspectives from which this phenomenon may be looked at also point to as many possible reasons for the change in the social relations between people and their needs, where the centrality of the individual - and their hedonistic/materialistic simplification in post-industrial society - is one of the traits commonly recognised by sociology, economy, politics and technology. The essay aims at investigating the formal features and the tools through which this new empathic process of interaction manifests itself, between men and artifacts, where the 'superficial layer' represents the main 'place' of formal expression. The assumption is centred upon the enhanced meaning of the surface of things, a support that seems to satisfy the materialistic need to establish a multi-sensory interaction between individuals and artifacts - using new materials, tools and processes, often strictly linked to confidence in the evolution of the technological world. Indeed, the latter appears to be

Figure 1.
Cover Rassegna n. 73 "Ri-vestimenti", Editrice Compositori, 1998, Bologna.

increasingly pervasive of human activities, in agreement with the assumptions that currently consider it more as an end in itself than as a means (Galimberti, 2000). In this text, the term 'empathy' is used in relation to 'abstraction': it is observed how a renewed figuration of artifacts and their surface has once again become the recurrent expressive and linguistic code. As a matter of fact, the figure seems suitable to the fast, compulsive consumption of our times. Through the text, the intention is to highlight this new supremacy of empathy, as the aesthetic field of figuration and mimesis, in opposition to the wide aesthetic field of abstraction and to a more 'laboured' conceptualisation of aesthetic content.

Over the last few years, the surface of things, although increasingly reduced in its dimension, has gone beyond the role of a medium, stratifying numerous meanings. It can be said that many of Italo Calvino's premonitions - lightness, rapidity, multiplicity - regarding the third Millennium are becoming real, in the ways and contents through which we perceive the objects around us and value them.

It is necessary to underline the context in which the reflections presented in this text emerged. They are drawn from two different settings: research experience carried out as the editor of the *Rassegna* section for *Domus* magazine over the years 2013-2016 and the investigation of some important design experiences.

In relation to the first reference context, it must be noted that since its foundation, *Domus* magazine has devoted a special section, called *Rassegna*, to a reasoned and annotated selection of materials and products for the human habitat. The products presented are mainly the result of research and innovation on the part of cutting-edge or emerging companies operating within the multi-faceted areas of living space - from product design, to furniture, finishes and construction components. This selection is a sort of 'photography' of formal and expressive changes and dominant topics, starting from the continuous renewal of company catalogues of products, components and systems for our living space. It therefore represents a meaningful 'test' to understand the more or less stable, recurrent aesthetic features and design themes, over increasingly shorter periods of time. From the first magazine subtitle, *Architettura e arredamento dell'abitazione moderna in città e in campagna* (*Architecture and Décor of the Modern Home in the City and in the Country*) to *Domus. Arte della casa* (*Domus. The Art of the Home*) and *I Quaderni* (*Notebooks*) in the 1940s and 1950s, to the sections on how to 'Set up a home', topics related to the 'ways' of living the newly-developing modern home were given special attention in the magazine contents. Through seemingly 'minor' topics, the close relationship between innovation and production - industrial and artisanal alike - and the opportunities to formally and aesthetically transform the environment and the quality of domestic life were documented. The opening texts, which I started editing in 2013 and are represented here in a partially revised form, had the precise goal of reflecting on the relations between the evolution of production, technology and materials

Figure 2.
Opening pages essay Section Rassegna, by Spartaco Paris.

and the relevant implications on the language of products and their form.

From this special observation point, it was actually possible to notice, firstly, the primacy of the representative function of contemporary living space, over other meanings; and secondly, the prevailing formal characterisation of the surface of artifacts, which stimulates the broadest sensory sphere and the tendency to favour new figurativeness over modern-rooted abstraction.

Im Anfang war die Bekleindung ('In the beginning was cladding') - indeed, in 1898, even Adolf Loos himself, in *Das Prinzip der Bekleidung,* (*The Principle of Cladding*), based on the studies by Semper, claimed that the true architect always thought in terms of skin, as the surface itself conditions the reactions of those living inside it. It is useful to underline - based precisely on reflections resulting from ob-servations of meaningful samples of products presented in the magazine over three years - an element that from a formal and a productive point of view characterises and is common to the multiplicity of products for our contemporary living space - in spite of the differences: today, architectural finishes, as has happened before at other times in history, are characterised by figures and environments, rather than form, increasingly moving away from abstraction. The recurrent and once again customary presence of figures, natural references, small- or large-sized ornaments and decorations, calls for a reflection on this phenomenology; this ranges from a detail in texture to the finishing elements in our interiors, to the surfaces which attri-bute expressive features to contemporary buildings, in a sort of new - unconscious?- reference to a materialist and naturalistic matrix in relation to the look of artifacts.

Surfaces and the search for pleasure support the current tendency towards indi-vidual narcissism, attributing meanings and desires to objects that go beyond the merely functional and/or representative scope.

Borrowing from Wilhelm Worringer's psychology of style (Worringer, 1909), em-pathy is once again an effective condition - today mainly derived from marketing strategies applied to products for the living space - concerning the formal charac-terisation of contemporary artifacts. The fast pace of life today requires formal solu-tions with an easy impact, where 'aesthetic enjoyment' is immediate and not linked to slow contemplation or conceptual references.

In this sense, abstraction - identified by Worringer as the opposite of empathy - is a minor field of design investigation, often relegated in a simplistic way to mini-malistic stylistic features or presented in the form of a tactile and perceptive char-acterisation of surface materials, through the 'modern' categories of transparency, reflection, shine.

The whole world of the image, especially the 'moving image' in digital animation, tends to offer hyper-realistic aesthetic simulacra, expanded mimesis, altered nature: this is the world of sensory stimuli in which we are immersed daily, a long way off

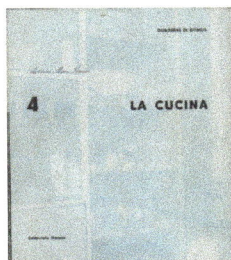

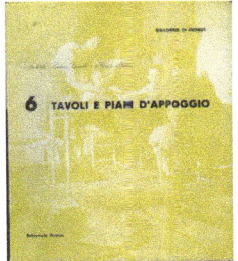

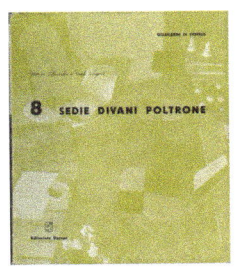
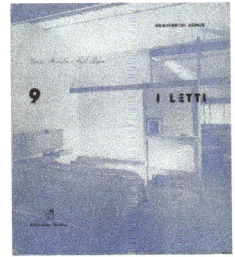

Figure 3.
Covers of Quaderni di Domus, 1945-1954,
series edited by Lina Bo and Carlo Pagani,
Editoriale Domus.

from the abstract modernity that we are, on the other hand, becoming less and less used to. Against the backdrop of this return to a new Epicurean materialism, it is possible to explain the reason for the infinite widening of a post-industrial landscape made of figures, surfaces and forms. Through other production techniques, they still hark back to naturalistic icons and simulacra. Today, basic morphemes and figures may be reproduced through endless, process-based digital algorithms, explicitly renewing a figurative repertoire, reinstating the impulse to imitate nature. The result, however, is a long way from art and not always interesting: tiles printed with leaves, arabesque decorations, naturalist and repeated patterns. This recurring approach may express the desire for a new intimacy in the relationship with things, the expectation and the pleasure of a human relationship - rather than a merely functional, or even a humanistic one - with objects.

"Everyday products are used, seen, touched. The tactile and expressive qualities of materials are important means of communication, and ask for a hands-on design process, an intense exploration of textures that appeal to the human scale. By means of its language and employment of techniques, good design expresses both the zeitgeist and a deep awareness of the past."

(Jongerius & Schouwenberg, 2015).

It is not coincidence that in the field of product design, textile design has recently acquired huge importance among countless contemporary design products. In this sense, issue No. 10 of *I Quaderni di Domus*, edited by Cini Boeri and Carlo Pagani from 1945 until 1954, dedicated to home curtains, was a forerunner. In this 'Supplements', an apparently 'minor', furniture-specific topic, is treated with the same importance, accuracy and attention as any typical design and architecture topic, by investigating its forms and design techniques.[3]

More recently, the topic of 'textile' surfaces has featured in many formal achievements and products of furniture and furnishings, beyond the specific upholstery sector: it is to be found often in 'intermediate' fields, between architecture and design, such as in Sevil Peach's alcoves for Vitra's office spaces, or in the Bouroullec's chromatic experiments in Textile Field carpets, exhibited at The London Design Festival in 2011, in the multiple tactile surfaces of Urquiola's designs and in the Valentino Boutiques by David Chipperfield - creating curtain effects using plaster reliefs - and even in the specific themes of textile design, such as the work of Hella Jongerius or Muller Van Severen, among others. The Dutch designer currently has a special role - being responsible for Vitra's choice of fabrics and textures for the upholstery products in their catalogue, in addition to designing the coordinated 'image' of upholstery and furnishings for KLM's Business class areas.

Textile surface designs (Carullo, Pagliarulo, 2013) acquire the technical form and contents common to the art of manufacturing. The actions of folding, sewing, weaving, layering - typical of 'textile' design - are exactly like design operations carried

Figure 4.
Detail of Bemolle e Diesis, sound-absorbing objects,
Design by Alessandro Mendini for Caimi Brevetti.
Salone del Mobile 2015

DAR AL JINAA

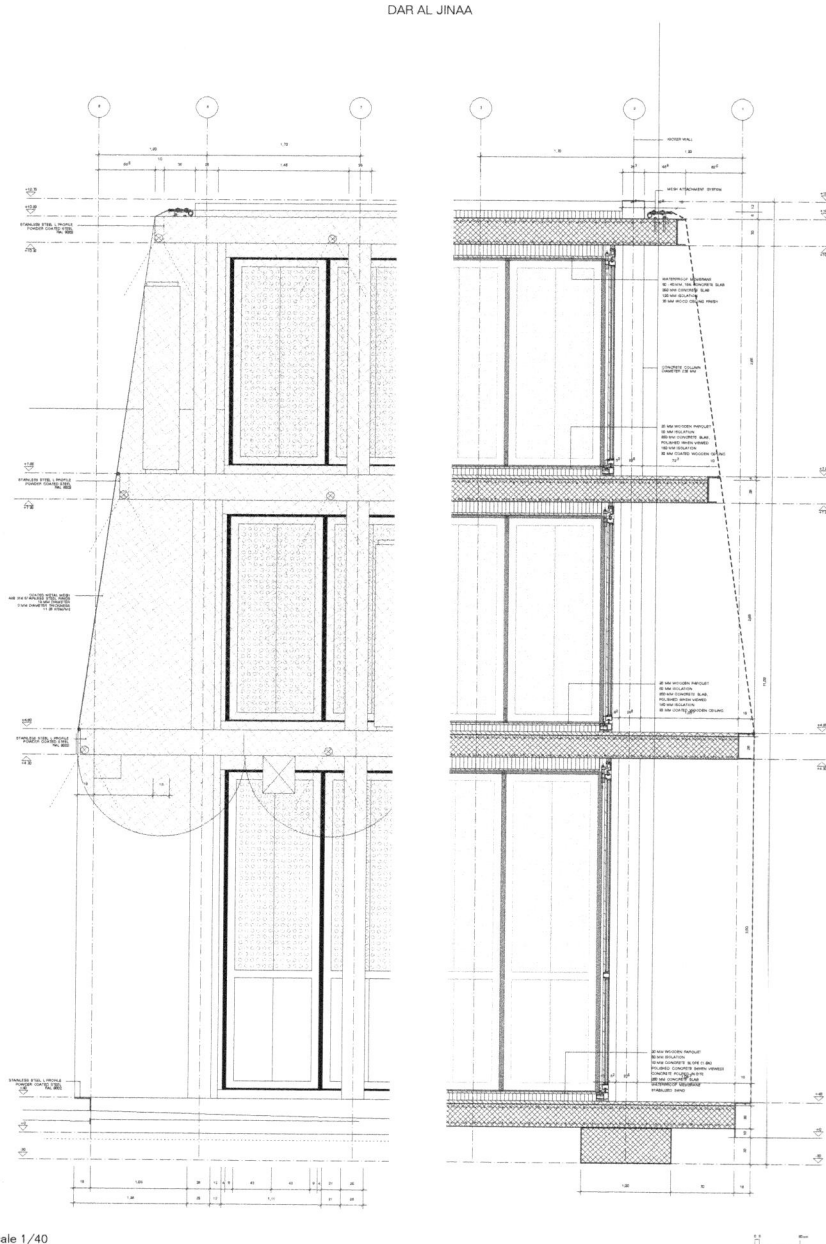

Scale 1/40

Figure 5a / 5b.
"*The building looks like a woman wearing a hijab. The stainless mesh skin hung from the top erases the sense of the building's mass, and appears like a stage curtain in a music hall.*"
(Go Hasegawa).
Centres for traditional music 2012 - 2018 / Muharraq (Dar Al ¬Jinaa)
Office Kersten Geers David Van Severen

out on 'thicknesses' in architecture, like the structured assembly of planes and lines.

It is possible to identify many meaningful experiences related to the design of up-holstery surfaces: from major companies in the textile industry (such as Kvadrat) to those working in the field of upholstery for living spaces, involving famous or emerging designers in their projects. Such experiences are centred upon the su-perficial implications of the wrapping of objects, therefore on the ability to trigger interactive mechanisms involving the senses beyond the visual sphere, the preferred choice of an idealist and modern culture. The wide variety of aesthetic results con-cerns artifacts on all scales in architecture, from micro (products) to mega (prod-ucts) : the field of investigation in surface upholstery patterns has been extended to the tactile features of elements, harking back to the 'textile' nature of artifacts that evoke Central European styles (Ursprung, 2005, Beccu, Paris, 2008).

The immediate reference, in the best scenarios, is the tectonics of surfaces and deco-rations in our living space, where textile aspects mix with plastic forms; assembly techniques and moulding - both digital and physical - define new aesthetic and ex-pressive characteristics, typical of the 'art of manufacturing'.

> *"To speak more generally, the ultimate goal of technology, the telos of techne, is to replace a natural world that's indifferent to our wishes - a world of hurri-canes and hardships and breakable hearts, a world of resistance - with a world so responsive to our wishes as to be, effectively, a mere extension of the self."*
> *(Franzen, 2011)*

Franzen's prophecy stemmed from the acknowledgement, experienced personally by the US writer with his Blackberry smartphone, of our obsessive relationship with smartphones and devices, like prosthetic limbs and extensions of our bodies. Immersed in the rapid acceleration of information technology, we have been as-sailed, in our daily routines, by actions that hyper-stimulate our senses - especially the touch, subjected to a rapid extension of its role in interactions between men and artifacts.

These interfaces - in which all the sensory implications of objects are concentrated - determine, together with form, a need for pleasure, a value that nowadays seems to be prevalent in the multitude of objects we move and live amongst.

Ever since the first modern educational experiences of the preparatory Bauhaus de-sign courses by J. Albers[4], the characteristics of materials and their surfaces (consis-tency, colour and shape) were linked to the psychology of perception, anticipating contemporary themes - such as interaction, empathy, skin and surfaces, the complex and accurate means establishing the multi-sensory relationship between man and artifact and between body and work. These experiences have, over time, been con-firmed by the points of view, among others, of Bruno Munari, Tomás Maldonado and Giovanni Anceschi, in the field of basic design.

Figure 6.
Textile Field, Design by Ronan Bouroullec Erwan Bouroullec for Kvadrat,
The London Design Festival September 2011

Maldonado himself recently acknowledged the 'return' to a new figuration - of easier empathy - observing the new, disrupting dominance of figurative representation and visual perception over abstraction, partly explaining it as based on the role of digital technology (Obrist, 2010).

It is about observing the extent to which the role played by the surface of objects, spaces and the artificial environment surrounding us, has at this time accentuated its formal characterisation over the definition of all the elements that are able to stimulate the sensory sphere of perception. Today we are witnessing the rule of the creation of 'spatial limits' over the creation of space itself. Within this discourse, the role of surfaces and design research into its endless features are fertile topics, impacting not only the specific scale of interior architecture and furniture design, but also the relationship between buildings and urban space, where the theme of 'decoration' acquires new values, updating the original ones.

We observe how the world of material and production techniques - thanks mainly to digitalisation and miniaturisation processes - are responding in a reactive manner to such stimulations and formal tendencies: multiplicity and loss of consistency seem to be specific features of contemporary materials. In other words, if on one hand, a material or component alone may satisfy multiple functions and needs, as performance increases there is a progressive reduction in weight and thickness, a loss of consistency compared to the solidity of the age-old materials we have inherited.

While the technological evolution of materials allows for a potential reduction in the amount needed to manufacture products, a new phenomenon, deriving from semiotics and transferred to the material aspect of artifacts, has been contributing to characterising its functions and most importantly the aesthetic experience, namely synaesthesia. Design and production techniques enable the replication - on any support through digital tools (e.g. digital printing) - of new 'images' of materials, not merely two-dimensional. This condition generates a tendency to accentuate the ambiguity of materials and their superficial consistency. As a matter of fact, surfaces acquire increasingly ambiguous features, simulating other materials, integrating perceptions and relations at times contradictory: hot/cold, soft/hard, smooth/rough. In the field of stone or ceramic products, to cite one of the most typical cases, many company catalogues feature ceramic tiles simulating other materials, with opposing sensory features, specifically creating synaesthetic effects in the user's perception. New surfaces therefore take on values where sensory and emotional aspects, amplified by the technology available, become the main design themes. In the field of wood-derived materials, upon request it is possible to manufacture a potentially infinite variety of surface finishes, resulting in effects that differ greatly from the original material. Production systems allow us to work on increasingly thinner thicknesses and take advantage of the boundless possibilities offered by digital printing to investigate surface finishing techniques. This is the case with photo-sensitive or

Figure 7.
Fabric-lined study boxes, Vitra office, Sevil Peach, Veil am Reihn, 2011

three-dimensional wallpaper, reconstituted wood textures, thermochromic cement, dynamic-configuration materials - to name just a few examples of surfaces offering uncommon sensory synaesthesiae, inspiring new ways of perceiving and experiencing reality and looking for simultaneous and overlapping stimuli.

Interest in the aesthetic features of cladding - the surface of artifacts - and the evolution of production techniques invite us to reconsider age-old theoretical and design paradigms, which are re-emerging today in a new form, going beyond a mere 'revival': in this context, it may be of interest to acknowledge the extent to which Semper's theories on the genesis of artifact design are relevant to modern times. First of all, a renewed 'tactile' characterisation of the objects of our times does indeed seem to confirm, at a later time, Semper's theories on the textile genesis of applied art (design) and architecture (Rykwert, 1990). For Semper, the principle of *Bekleidung* implied a common - textile - origin of all the arts, attributing a logical priority to ornament over structure. In Semper's system, major arts share the same formative principles as applied art (*Kunstgewerbe*) and supremacy is given to the representative component, which nowadays is empathy.

Second, it is possible to recognise the validity of those who claim that the world of techniques has more than a merely instrumental role in elaborating design forms. The recent *Sempering* exhibition, curated by Luisa Collina and Cino Zucchi, as part of the events by the XXI Triennale di Milano, was the perfect occasion to bring attention back to the influence of Gottfried Semper and his theory on the principle of cladding and to highlight the function of techniques in relation to the design concept, as part of the architecture-design dyad. The theme of his most famous publication, entitled *Der Stil* (*The Style*), was the reference to the 'necessary' relations between *ars* and techniques in design: in the four arts (textiles, ceramics, tectonics-carpentry and stereotomy), Semper had tried to define different ontological matrices of architecture itself, in a structuralist dialogue between plastics and tectonics, which today we may also find in the field of applied arts and design, where the production processes of the 4.0 industrial revolution inevitably refer to a model of customised production.

The field of techniques therefore appears essential once again in defining new investigations into form, in a two-fold aspect: on one hand - consistent with a process-based interpretation of the definition of form, it identifies in production not only the elements to verify formal schemes, but also a field for new morphological paradigms to be defined. For example, in the repetition of patterns generated by digital design tools (*Processing*, Arduino), we observe the renewed use of ornamental patterns based on traditional techniques. On the other hand, the field of digital techniques and three-dimensional modelling processes allows us to make a reference to rational mathematical parameters - therefore reproducible, based on any formal assumption. This creates a reciprocal relationship between art and production techniques, infinitely widening customisation possibilities to meet increasingly individual needs and desires.

Figure 8.
Detail of the Parthenon, Akropolis, Athens. Painted by Gottfried Semper, 1836. Archiv ETH Zurich.

Figure 9.
Cover of Wilhem Worringer, Abstraktion und Einfülung. Abstraction and Empathy.
A contribution to the Psychology of style. 1908.

It is a call for a new tectonics of forms and advanced methods of 'making and manufacturing' - no longer basic and taxonomic, as they were in Semper's times, but manifold and sophisticated: a return to techniques being once again a fertile ground for design development, where design can free itself from the contemporary misunderstanding that has reduced it to a 'concept' - at times even mystical - more typical of marketing, than of design work itself.

Design seems thus to revolve around the relationship between techniques and the preeminence of decoration - as the true, ultimate supremacy of the designer, and therefore centred around the surface of artifacts, where the representative component finds fertile ground in the empathy of the surface of things.

The text is a new revised version of the essay "The design of surfaces, between empathy and new figuration", written by the author for the The Design Journal, n. 20, 2017.

Notes

1. The 'sense-feel-think-act-relate' categories refer to the modes of interaction between man/inhabitant, space and objects. Starting from the category related to the evolution of marketing strategies and studies - such as in *Experiential Marketing: How to Get Customers to Sense, Feel, Think, Act, Relate to Your Company and Brands.* by B.H. Schmitt (New York, 1999) – the individual's 'experience' of space and artifacts has been at the core of studies investigating its characteristics, spanning from the psychology of perception, statistics and economics.. As far as 'inhabiting' is concerned, and its phenomenological relationship to the individual/inhabitant, - in *Dell'abitare. Corpi spazi oggetti immagini* ('On Inhabiting. Bodies spaces objects images') – Maurizio Vitta analyses the main characters who take part in inhabiting, including the individual's body who plays the leading role in relation to space.

2. 'I believe that the interior world deploys like a project: it can be mapped out and given form in terms of the architecture of stratification [...] In other words, film, architecture and clothing find a common point here as they 'stratify' on the surface of things. All three have the ability to shape a surface landscape that acts as a casing. They are our second skin, our sensory suit. They communicate our inner configuration and are the site of the dynamics of emotions.' Giuliana Bruno, Surface: Matters of Aesthetics, Materiality and Media, University of Chicago Press, Chicago 2014, p. 18.

3. The titles of the 11 *I Quaderni di Domus* were: Domus. Titles: 1. I libri nella casa (*The books in the home*, trans. Paris), Vito Ladis ed., 1945; 2. Gli studi nella casa. (*The studies in the home*, trans. Paris), Vittorio Gandolfi ed., 1945; 3. Camini. (*Fireplaces*, trans. Paris) , Mario Tevarotto ed, 1945; La cucina. (*The kitchen*, trans. Paris), Marco Zanuso ed., 1945; 5. L'illuminazione della casa. (*The lighting of house*, trans. Paris) Luigi Claudio Olivieri ed., 1946; 6. Tavoli e piani d'appoggio. (*Tables and supports*, trans. Paris), Luciano Canella e Renato Radici ed., 1948; 7. L'elemento verde e l'abitazione. (*The green element and the home*, trans. Paris), Luigi Figini ed., 1950; 8. Sedie, divani, poltrone. (*Chairs, sofas, armchairs*, trans. Paris), Vittorio Borachia e Carlo Pagani. 1950; 9. I letti. (*The beds*, trans. Paris) Vittorio Borachia e Carlo Pagani ed., 1951; 10. Le tende nella casa. (*The home curtains*, trans. Paris), Cini Boeri e Carlo Pagani, 1952; 11. I soggiorni. (*The living rooms*, trans. Paris), Vittorio Borachia e Carlo Pagani ed.,1954.

4. J. Albers in *Werklicher Formunterricht* (*Teaching Form Through Practice*, 1928) outlines an inductive and experiential learning path within the Preparatory Course to Bauhaus, through an experimentation, called *Materie*, on materials and their 'skin'. "This longstanding practice of neglecting the natural surface of materials makes it difficult to take up this multifaceted task of developing the finest possible feeling for the material. In order to concentrate the experience, we not only assemble materials in suites to seek relationships; we also create textures and factures, invent them, and then translate them into materials with different colors or hues; we substitute materials with related appearances for them; and we imitate them in drawings or paintings." English translation by Frederick Amrine, Frederick Horowitz, and Nathan Horowitz - Bauhaus 1928(..).

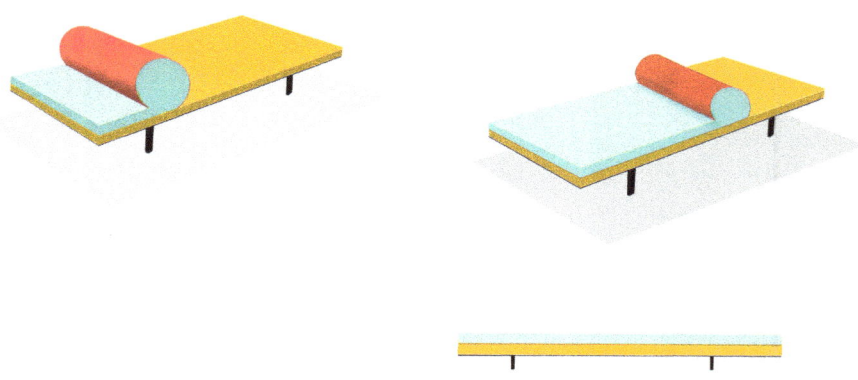

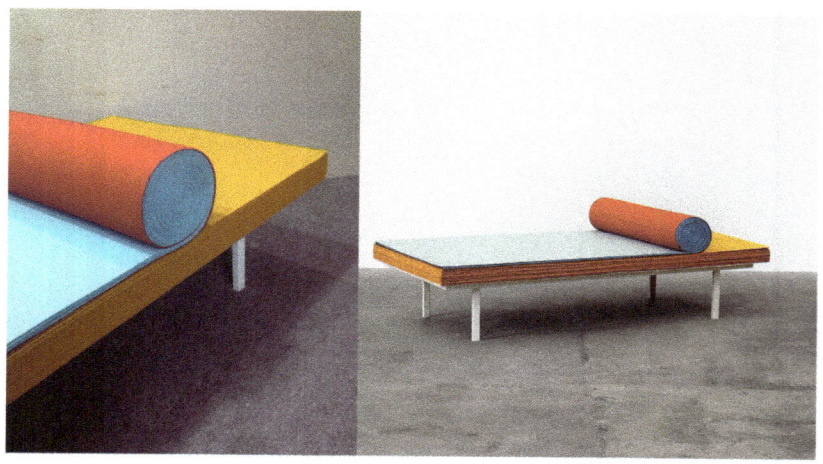

Figure 10.
Divina textile Bench, Muller Van Severen, drawings and photos, Kvadrat, 2014

Figure 11.
Colour trials and fabric swatches with matching buttons for two new versions of the Polder Sofa,
Design by Hella Jongherius for Vitra, 2005 and updated for 2015
Milan furniture Fair

L'architecture donne forme à l'eau,
les piliers donnent forme au lac,
comme la topographie en tant que structure
donne forme à l'eau, et dessine une rivière.

Une nouvelle rivière apparaît dans le lac.

Figure 12.
Junya Ishigami- Freeing Architecture, Foundation Cartier, Paris, 2018

Figure 13.
"Sempering", Mudec Museum, XXI Triennale, Milan, L. Collina, C. Zucchi curators, 2016

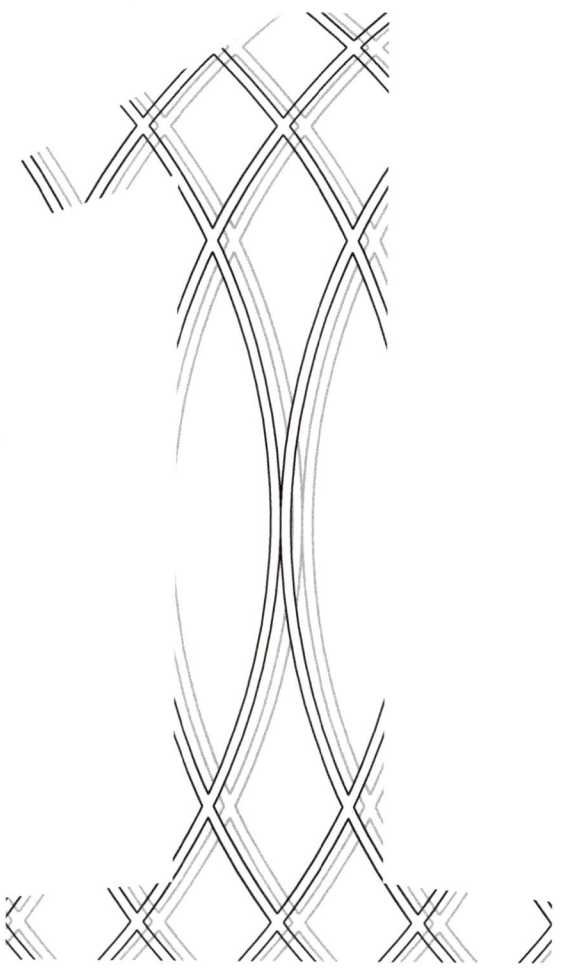

PART I
BUILDING / PRODUCTION
CHAPTER 1
MATERIALS AND SUSTAINABILITY IN DESIGN

1.1 Sustainable building

As early as the Second World War, a few isolated pioneers of modernism were attempting to rethink architecture, placing it in a harmonious relationship with nature. Another step in this direction was made in the 1970s, highlighted by the energy crisis: the value of sustainable building was promulgated by groups appertaining to environmentalist movements and for a long time it remained the preserve of specialists. It regarded a number of marginal aspects of buildings, where the physical-technical and environmental components were the weak 'theoretical basis' for guiding decisions and designs belonging to specialised niche construction. The results achieved, more related to technical aspects than convincing formal outcomes, relegated green design to something outside the architecture recognized by critics. In the early 1990s, the concept of sustainability gradually began to be more and more assimilated into the construction industry: the architects themselves who found in the technical side their own expressive medium, had their own way of rethinking the actual role of technology in an ecological approach, seeking new recognition in the field of building production, often by the use of prefixes - eco or bio - attributed to the term architecture.

This phase did not produce particularly meaningful architecture, apart from in a few rare cases, but had the advantage of enabling the progressive transfer of the value of sustainability into building regulations and, as a result, the market. Respect for green criteria has therefore become a legislative requirement, then a shared necessity and, only in part, a way of conceiving contemporary architecture. It has thus occurred that levels of energy and environmental performance have been redefined. Gradually we have begun to understand how building construction has a crucial role to play when weighing up the consumption of energy and other resources. A new awareness has emerged as to the need to use our resources both carefully and sparingly[1], not only to conserve our fragile world for future generations, but also for rethinking in general our existing built heritage, constructed at a time in which the economic model of growth guided production and management. Thus, green building can in western countries mean rebuilding while integrating environmental sustainability with social and economic; for emerging economies who are undergoing their own modernisation, it can mean rethinking approaches to urban and building development, gaining insights from the lessons and mistakes of European modernity. The construction industry, which even today does not have the impetus of mass production, except for building components, has all the tools for making products in a rational way from an economic point of view and efficient from an environmental point of view. Research in this field regards products throughout their entire cycle of production use-disposal-recycling. The issue is how to identify and carry out choices that begin, beyond the technical requirements that the market imposes, with a more conscious design approach, that combines craftsmanship with industry in an ethic that leads to fabricating and inhabiting new architecture.

From: *Domus* n. 1009 Gennaio / January 2017. Sustainable Building

1.2 Design and Sustainability

Over a period of forty years, the issue of the environment - in the sense of the impact of systems of production and consumption on the balance of ecosystems - has gone from belonging to a more pioneering, alternative dimension, to being considered a fundamental requisite of products and material goods.

The healthier and more advanced industrial organisations have assimilated the need to define overall production strategies that centre not just around the logics of profit but are based on an ethical principle that can establish sustainable industrial models for future generations. This journey has taken place in stages: starting with the first isolated situations in the 1970s, it wasn't until the early 1990s that the theory and study of sustainable development became a shared patrimony and the industrial world introduced the notion of compatibility with the environment into their manufacturing processes, capitalising on them as adding value rather than experiencing them as a constraint to be limited by. Over the last twenty years, environmentalist thinking has become more and more recognisable as a set of values and today it even sounds somewhat outdated to add the prefix eco or bio to terms that define the industrial product and the design development phase. Nowadays, any company that aspires to producing quality goods places sustainability among the basic requisites of the product, while the certification of 'environmental quality' has created a real market, aimed at classifying the eco-efficiency of every product. The actual boundaries of sustainability have been extended to the point of including the effects that we retain plausible within our behaviour of individuals and consumers (social sustainability) and the variable of costs and benefits of the production cycle, for which using smaller quantities of resources and producing less waste means saving money and generating profit (economic efficiency). Thus materials and products have become green and smart, communicating, through often reductive slogans, the intelligence and human rationality behind them and leading to defining a renewed capacity for design, production and management of the entire life cycle of a product. This phenomenon of responsibility towards a rational use of resources has found particularly fertile ground in contexts in which their scarcity has imposed forms of rationalisation, or also during periods of economic crisis such as that which occurred in Europe in the 2000s, that has led to a rethinking of models of development based on 'happy de-growth'[2]. This has stimulated the redefinition of local economic and productive supply-chains, to complement global ones and based on the recycling, reuse and salvage of materials and goods. But it has also led to the adoption of new behaviours, above all in 'poor' economies that have made use of their own natural tendency to design and produce in the face of scarcity of resources using simple materials that are easy to transform or salvage: these are unconscious testimonies of a post-industrial economy. The challenge of adopting a healthier economy of production now mainly regards the countries affected by new growth and economic development.

From: 2016 *Domus* n.1004 Luglio-Agosto/July-August 2016. Design and Sutainability

1.3 On the consistency and multiplicity of materials

The last of Italo Calvino's *Six Memos for the Next Millennium*, following the one on 'Multiplicity'[3], was to have been titled 'Consistency', with Herman Melville's Bartleby, the Scrivener as its subject-matter. It was never completed. This gap in many ways rings true with the loss of 'consistency' of the new millennium. Multiplicity and Consistency. Two paradigms, two qualities, which, if applied to the materials of architecture, lend themselves to a dialectic interpretation. Consistency is a value that brings us back to the idea of massiveness and permanence, reminiscent of the great, solid architecture of the past - built to last, to be stratified and to age. Multiplicity on the other hand leads us - true to Calvino's prophetic intuitions - into the materials of our millennium. Increasingly sophisticated and, thanks to technologies, slowly but steadily evolving, these materials offer ever more efficient and multiple performances in progressively thinner gauges and sections.

If we think of the evolution of glazed materials, we can observe a steadily reduced consistency of sections, together with a larger number of functions/performances provided by a single material. Andrea Deplazes[4] has represented this phenomenon with an iconic analogy drawn from aeronautics. He compares a lunar astronaut's suit - a heavy armour made of many layers, each performing a specific function - with the ultra-light 'suit' for Mars: a light skin with just a few multifunctional layers. The evolution of materials is leading us - also in the name of the environmental paradigm - towards a loss of physical and material consistency in favour of an increasing immaterial efficiency. With building materials, the process is slower, relating everlastingly to the necessary function of *firmitas* in architecture and to the new paradigm of sustainability. These factors are creating two recognisable scenarios. On the one hand, we have a massive new solidity of architectural materials, ranging - to mention a few consolidated examples - from new structural wood panels (CLT or Xlam) to load-bearing and thermal blocks in honeycomb brick, or to the numerous industrial variants of autoclaved concrete.

The second scenario concerns architecture according to the evolution of Semper's '*Prinzip der Bekleidung*', made of strata and each with a specific performance, used to clad structures while concealing or representing them. In this latter situation the ancient building, with its capacity to 'age', is materially 'superseded' by a building with parts and elements to be replaced when broken and in which invention on the aesthetic connotation of 'bodywork' is increasingly relevant. At the top of this consistency/multiplicity dyad is the duration of the architectural product, its reaction to time, its aptitude to last and to change, or to be substituted once its ever-shorter life cycle is over. If durability in architecture becomes once again necessary in our contemporaneity, and if we can sustainably deal with our immense built heritage to be restored, recycled and improved, then material consistency will find a renewed place in industry for architecture.

From: *Domus* n. 974 Novembre / November 2013. Materials

1.4 Even the materials became smart

We spoke of multiplicity and a loss of consistency as being specific characteristics of contemporary materials. In other words, a single material or component can respond to a plurality of demands and functions on one hand, and on the other we see increased performance corresponding to progressive reduction in the weight and thickness of materials, a loss of consistency compared to the solidity of the ancient materials handed down to us. In current times, we are even able to attribute intelligence to materials, so it is not surprising that a new phenomenon now sits alongside the multiplicity and ductility of materials: the ambiguity, not to mention the concealment, of many new yet well-established materials. To give an example of the most evident, in the field of stoneware and ceramic, many manufacturers are offering ceramic tiles that visually (but not yet tactilely) resemble wood.

They are offering increasingly easy maintenance and cleaning; environmentally friendly production processes; and formidable performance. In the field of wood-derived materials, a potentially infinite array of surface finishes can be supplied on demand, far removed from the original characteristics of wood. This condition accompanies growing attention for qualities that have established market value: eco-compatibility of materials, reduced consumption of non-renewable resources, and the re-use of manufacturing waste. To address the complex issue of sustainability, material processing technology is being developed through a number of paradoxes.

We are witnessing a gradual separation between performance (including visual perception and aesthetics in general) and the intrinsic characteristics of materials: a kind of separation/concealment between *Kern Form* and *Kunst Form*. The development of manufacturing technologies makes it possible for the intrinsic characteristics of each material (*Kern Form*) to correspond less and less to the final aesthetic result (*Kunst Form*).

Throughout history, technical skill in working material resources, first through craft, then industry, has shaped them into other materials and then components for both architecture and the applied arts. This came about by following a mostly coherent line in bringing out the individual characteristics of each material: stone was treated and worked as such, so were clay, wood and metal. Stuccoes had the possibility of assuming multiple forms. With synthetic materials and the advent of plastics and polymers - similarly to what happened when reinforced concrete came to building construction - we have had to search out the aesthetic attributes of materials that in themselves are amorphous and, at the same time, able to take on any appearance.

Recently in a European airport I happened to touch a column that looked like it was made from skillfully antiquated brick only to hear the hollow sound of a plastic prop.

Today this is even happening to materials that are endowed with their own characteristics and their own potential beauty, all in the name of an increasingly critical market economy, where the need to satisfy individual desires increasingly concerns the sphere of appearances rather than reality. Once again Calvino was right to invoke 'consistency' for the new millennium, in the last of his *Memos*[5].

From: *Domus* n. 985 Novembre / November 2014. Materials

Notes

1. Vittorio Magnago Lampugnani, *Domus MILLE*, March 2016.

2. See Serge Latouche, *Petit traité de la décroissance sereine.* 1001 Nuits. Paris. France

3. Italo Calvino, *Six Memos for the Next Millennium*, Harvard University Press, Cambridge, Massachusetts 1988.

4. Andrea Deplazes, *Sustainability. Fundamentals of Architecture*, in A. Deplazes (ed.), *Constructing Architecture. Materials, Processes, Structures, a Handbook, Birkhäuser*, p. 282.

5. Italo Calvino *ibidem.*

Figure 14.
Museum of Natural History, Berlin, Renovation project by Diener & Diener Architekten).
Detail of the facade, with integration in pre-moulded concrete.

Figure 15.
Composite re-cycled materials - paperstone experiment.
Furniture design through composite eco-materials: an in-depth analysis of PaperStone features.
Student: Lorenzo Santini.
Supervisor: Spartaco Paris.
Master of Science in Product Design, Sapienza Università di Roma, 2017

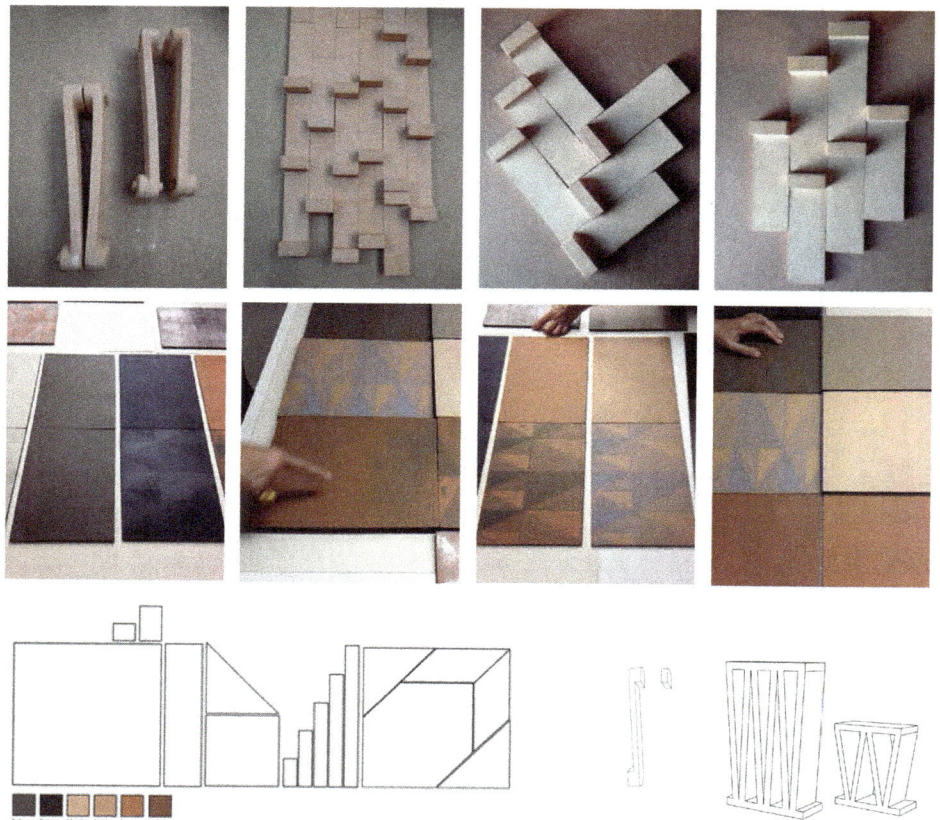

Figure 16.
Sustainable process of clay production:
The collection Tierras by Patricia Urquiola for Mutina.
Drawings and production phases of tiles, made in unglazed stoneware.

Figure 17.
Composite re-cycled materials:
Metalleido honeycomb panel Furniture design through composite eco-materials,
applied research in collaboration with Abet Laminati.
Master of Science in Product Design, Design Studio V,
coordinator: prof. Spartaco Paris, prof. Francesco Romeo
Sapienza Università di Roma, 2017-2019

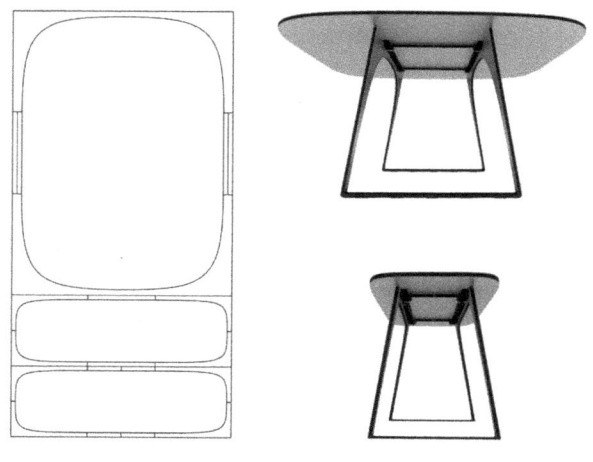

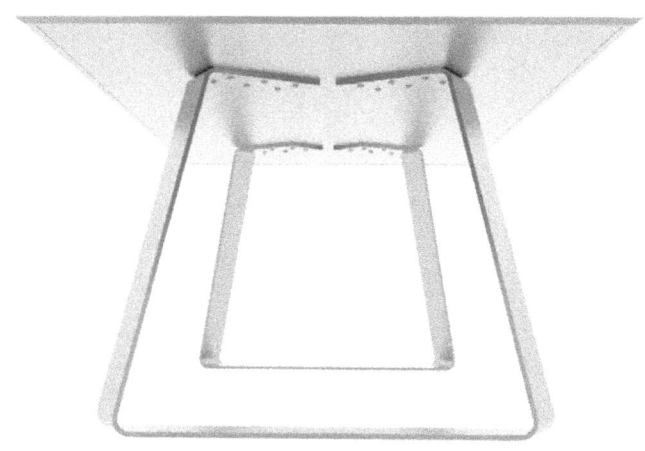

Figure 18.
Composite re-cycled materials:
Metalleido honeycomb panel Furniture design through composite eco-materials,
applied research in collaboration with Abet Laminati.
Master of Science in Product Design, Design Studio V,
coordinator: prof. Spartaco Paris, prof. Francesco Romeo
Sapienza Università di Roma, 2017-2019

Figure 19.
Durability: the other way to sustanabiliy. 20-06™ collection,
Design by Foster + Partners, for Emeco, 2013

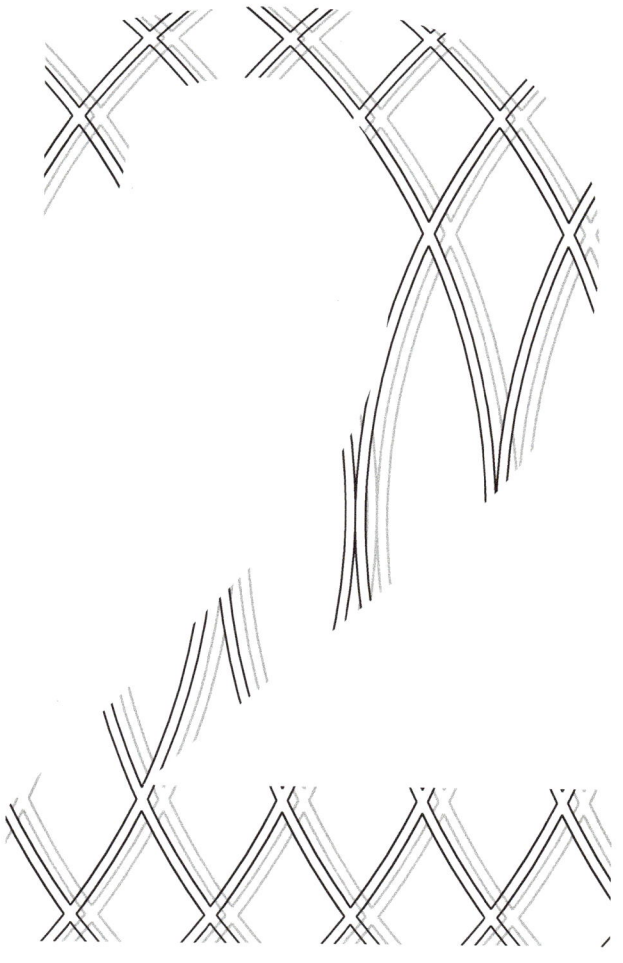

PART I
BUILDING / PRODUCTION
CHAPTER 2
ENVELOPES/SURFACES/ FACADES

2.1 Architectural envelope: the 'thickness' of surfaces

Joseph Rykwert[6] quotes Adolf Loos's dictum 'In the beginning was cladding' ('*Am Anfang war die Bekleidung*') in order to underline the supremacy of surface over structure, in keeping with Semper's theory on the 'textile' origins of architecture. According to Semper, cladding can be related to the act of stitching (*nath*) as well as to necessity (*noth*, the Greek αναγχη) or the knot (*knote*), intended as a primary technical symbol.

In the case of the building envelope or vertical enclosure, architectural cladding encompasses the dual and contrasting roles of decoration and protection that, along with 'modesty', absolve the need - thus the necessity - for man to clothe himself and similarly for architecture to manifest itself through its cladding.

The relationship between the need for protection (and modesty) and the virtues of decoration is one of the opposing poles in a dialectic that over recent years has witnessed the supremacy of decoration, stimulating needs rather than satisfying them as such. As Vittorio Gregotti[7] observed, beauty, fame, wealth and allure are the trademarks of fashion, yet they have also struck and seduced architecture, its forms and especially facades and surfaces with regards to a more immediate manifestation. Through the domain of images, building facades have proved to be the most immediate and also the most fertile place for exploration, representation and communication.

The paradigm of sustainability has made this exploration into the architecture of the building envelope and its representation even richer and more complex. The shared environmental ethic of the 'market' has become the consolidated - already partly consumed - paradigm determining effects on the architecture of the building envelope that fall into at least three categories: 1) in opaque surfaces, the definitive split between structure and enclosure, separated by ever-thicker layers of insulation, for architectural envelopes that are increasingly hyper-insulated; this has the effect of restoring the supremacy of architectural cladding over structure with echoes of Semper that are not always conscious; 2) in surfaces that are largely transparent (curtain walls and glazed facades), promoting the reduction of the relationship between frame and glazing with the increased performance and functions of glass building components and similar products; 3) the diffusion of intermediary components and systems for facades that combine layers of elements that are neither totally opaque nor completely transparent: *brise-soleils*, diaphragms, grilles and filters now define a consolidated range of looks and solutions for facades that use cladding as a further layer of drapery, that filter and modulate the flow of air and light between the inside and outside of the building. These offer visual effects and a level of expression that is mostly geared towards a spectral architecture, which is often ephemeral and quickly consumed as an icon.

The technology of systems and components for architectural envelopes contributes to determining architectural language, offering contrasting approaches.

The first and more prevalent tends to affirm a possible consistence of architecture with the industrial product, a 'machine', an object to sell, consume, conserve with pre-programmed cycles of maintenance, modify, substitute and demolish. The second - relating to envelopes of a more conservative type - tends to reintroduce a possible solid and permanent side to architecture, which relates to sustainability as an object transmissible to future generations, able to encompass 'solidity' and sturdiness.

From: *Domus* n. 977 Febbraio / February 2014. Facades

2.2 Facades. On the usefulness of a modern taxonomy of architecture fundamentals

Of the 15 architectural elements used by Koolhaas and the Harvard Graduate School of Design to analyse architecture in the exhibition *Elements* at the 14th Architecture Biennial in Venice, the one that played the biggest role and was ascribed the greatest relevance, like a veritable 'metonymy' of architecture itself, was the facade[8] .

According to the theory developed by Gottfried Semper in the 1800s on the 'textile' origin of architecture, the facade shouldn't have just a decorative role, but reveal the architectural character of the building itself, its capacity to communicate. Semper's theory in fact sanctions a break between meaning and construction, between the primacy of the cladding and the notion of what the structure represents.

The technological evolutions of the 20th Century, however, contributed to establishing the lengthy dominance of the facade-surface - degenerating into 'facadism' - although this was made gradually more complex by the inclusion of additional layers for functional purposes. Having surpassed - for technological reasons - the classical syntax of a composition of architectural elements (opening, wall, loggia, cornice, base, crown), over the years we have witnessed a process whereby the formal investigation of facades has progressively reduced them to skin-like decorative surfaces, characterised by patterns and textures, potentially repeated ad *infinitum* - that are recognizable as being in a particular architect's style, or inspired by it - just like the world of fashion.

In recent years however, signs have begun to appear that demonstrate, by virtue of a slow renewal of the civic function of architecture and the emergence of the 'paradigm' of sustainability, that the role of the facade - and the architectural envelope in general - has been newly invested with the function of creating the useful conditions for a well-designed interior and reducing energy consumption, in ways that are as natural and economic as possible. This new role is loaded with symbolic and representative content.

The layers of the contemporary architectural envelope can be seen to pursue two opposing trends. In the first, the facade is articulated in systems with numerous mono-functional layers, each with a specific purpose. In this case there is a separation between cladding and structure, between skin and skeleton, following the theory of a 'textile origin' of architecture. The second trend instead centres around research that has its origins in masonry construction and architectural mass - even if built today with slender walls made from load-bearing timber panels. The stratification of the facade is achieved with multifunctional single-layered systems. This second approach tends to define single-layered systems of enclosure able to perform multiple functions using single components (for example honeycomb blocks, concrete blocks, load-bearing timber systems) delegating once again to the surface material the role of finish.

These two trends demonstrate the great dialectic around the very idea of architecture: the first, in continuity with the modernist interpretation of the building as a 'machine' - now ecological - sees it as a product, with a life-cycle and an elimination phase; in the second, the building has its own specific 'nature', with a lifespan that should be extended for as long as possible.

From: *Domus* n. 994 Settembre / September 2015. Facades

2.3 The building skin and its fragile consistency

Many, only seemingly obvious, analogies have been made between the cladding of a building and human skin[9].

The one real difference is that human skin has no structural role whereas, instead, this can be the case with buildings.

Like our epidermis, the skin of a building has two main functions: one is protection, stopping water getting in and filtering air coming from outside; the other is representative, concurring along with the body to define the architectural expression of the building, just as skin characterises people's outer appearance[10].

Like skin, the building envelope is also not immune to the effects of ageing. As architects of our time, we know that in the coming years we increasingly have to address the use of existing buildings, redesigning them, taking care of them, renovating them and when it is inevitable, demolishing them and replacing them. It is likely that this will be the principal activity of architects over the course of the millennium we have recently begun.

Our 'modern' architectural heritage, the built environment of the 20th Century, was not initially conceived to be long-lasting. The myth of the *'machine à habiter'* led to interpreting parts of a building as industrial components, associated with short life cycles, imagining that later generations would design continually-evolving ways of living. In short, modern machine-building was conceived to be replaced by newer methods and newer materials. But this 'replacement' process did not fully take place and so the built patrimony of the 20th Century has ended up being rather inadequate in terms of meeting current needs for use, comfort and safety.

The building envelope is a crucial part of this patrimony; here lie some of the major innovations of the modern building. As a result, the skin of buildings constructed as from the last century - particularly delicate because it is thin, light or made with non-traditional materials - often ends up failing to meet new demands in terms of function and protection. If we accept the idea of the building-machine also for the fragile architecture built in the second half of the 20th Century, the best, easiest and most sustainable care would consist of continuous and low-cost programmed maintenance, as with the automobiles that we use every day. Obsession with energy-saving has furthermore identified in the building envelope one of the major places for therapeutic intervention on buildings, sometimes taking extraordinary measures.

For buildings that belong to relevant and recognised cultural heritage, even today it is quite complex to balance the needs for energy saving with those of cultural heritage protection and this requires an awareness of public interest. From this point of view, the 'modern' building provides a great opportunity to intervene in lengthening the life of fragile buildings, in other words offering them a second life. It is not a case of working just on the make-up of modern buildings, the results of which, as with plastic surgery, would alter natural proportions and balance. Redesigning modern construction requires a deep knowledge of what is wrong and a broad design culture that does not just succumb to the promises made by technology.

From: *Domus* n. 1015 Luglio–Agosto / July–August 2017. Envelopes

2.4 Fenestration

In architecture, windows are the construction elements that enable air and light to enter the rooms we inhabit and as such, have always made an important contribution to maintaining a healthy living environment.

From a purely semantic point of view, right from the very origins of architecture their nature has evolved in two ways: in sculpted, masonry architecture they are 'holes' in the perimetral, structural mass of the building. In the evolution of flexible-wood architecture, 'fabric' if we want to use the terms defined by Gottfried Semper, they are part of a wall like a membrane (*Die Wand)*, performing a representative as well as a protective function in architecture. As they are no longer bound in a reciprocal relationship with the structure, they can gradually extend to the point of dissolving into transparent walls. With the evolution of modern technology, the window has increased in size, thus enabling a new kind of relationship to be established between interior and exterior spaces, transforming the tectonic relationship between the original constituent parts. An example of this can be seen in Kenneth Frampton's comments regarding the complex technology designed by Mies van der Rohe in building the large windows for the Lange and Esters houses at Krefeld, both made from brick. The matter of the window construction is highlighted in the critical analysis of the complex structural logic of the house. 'Mies's engineer, Ernst Walther, complained at length about the economic and technical problems involved in achieving such large spans in brick openings. In a letter to Mies, he complained of his liberal use of Reiner [sic] beams and other elaborate structural devices. However, such spans enabled Mies to provide large picture windows in both the Esters and Lange residences'[11] .

In times in which the comfort of our indoor environment has been entrusted exclusively to mechanical systems, the progressive increase in the dimensions of transparent openings has led to a progressive increase in levels of energy consumption in buildings. Over the last twenty years, measures have been put in place that, in a shared and holistic way, have focused on combining the need for a healthy indoor environment with a reduction in the levels of energy consumption. The modern myth of the metal window with the slenderest of frames was placed under threat by these new demands for comfort and efficiency in buildings, in which windows were considered the 'weakest' construction element.

Research into ensuring ever-higher performance and guaranteeing a reduction in heat loss has led to an increase in the number of layers of glass and their efficiency, along with a new 'consistency' for fixed and moving frames, in order to meet higher standards of strength and water tightness: other components have been integrated into the window, able to modulate the ingress of light and heat, shading elements, blinds and screens that contribute to defining new, short-lived architectural languages, in the search for its difficult consistency.

From: *Domus* n. Febbraio / February 2016. Frames and Sunshadings

2.5 Frames

The English word 'frame', when referring to doors and windows, embodies a 'poetic' as well as a technical meaning, a more precise term to express the aesthetic role of doors and windows as architectural elements beyond the merely functional.

In Italian a picture-frame is a '*cornice*', while a door-frame is a '*telaio*', - only our word 'frame' also implies a surround for landscapes and spaces.

It may be useful to consider the fact that in recent decades, when it comes to doors and windows, their aesthetic development has followed a process of reduction. In the beginning it was industrial manufacturing that affected the performance and functional efficiency of buildings. The need to reduce energy losses has provided a significant motivation for seeking better performance from the building envelope, and this has had a considerable effect on windows, with frames becoming more complex with additional layers of glazing and more sophisticated components articulated in functional layers, each given over to a different function. All of this has meant that the technical aspect has prevailed over the form, with some exceptions: for example, the 'all glass' systems where, thanks to the technological development of adhesives, it is possible for the glazed surfaces to extend beyond the frames on the outside, reducing the thickness of the frames and creating a '*pan de verre*' effect for the windows. In the case of internal doors, whose performance requirements are less complex, we have seen a proliferation of 'flush' solutions in which design has newly converted the frames into slender lines. The diffusion of these systems has led to a reduction of the presence of the door within the interior, integrating into the wall and designing only an elementary shape.

Meanwhile today, in terms of style, contemporary research in design and industrial production seems to lean, therefore, towards the cautious and somewhat homologated direction of dissimulating or reducing the visual presence of doors and windows while industrial patents mainly regard the functional aspects. If we look at the past, however, it was the presence and 'dimension' of the frames around doors and windows that provided the decoration in a house, as well as resolving the junction between the wall and frame in an effective way.

If we look back in history, there was a phase in which, via new formal paradigms derived from industry, new languages were dreamed up for doors and windows: the age of the heroic patents of Jean Prouvé[12]. It was within the world of industry and a positive notion of progress, that the great 'French tinsmith' - to use the words of historian François Chaslin - continually sought to innovate the form as well as function of every component - from the chair to the entire house - inventing new forms, materials and production processes .

His metal panels and riveted doors with portholes, that today seem like true archaeological finds, are veritable testimonies of a 'modern poetics of technical objects'.

To Prouvé we owe a new syntax and lexicon that became the archetypes of a marriage between architecture, design and industry, that still today remain an unsurpassed example for contemporary masters and the architects of the future.

From: *Domus* n. 1011 Marzo / March 2017. Systems of enclosure

Notes

6. Joseph Rykwert, 'L'architettura è tutta nella superficie. Semper e il principio del rivestimento' / 'Architecture lies in the surface. Semper and the cladding principle', in *Rassegna*, Ri-vestimenti, n. 73, 1998, p. 20.

7. Vittorio Gregotti, 'Editoriale', in Rassegna, 'Ri-vestimenti', n. 73, 1998, p.19

8. Alejandro Zaera-Polo, S. Trüby, Rem Koolhaas, Amo, Harvard Graduate School of Design, Irma Boom, 'Façade', *Elements of Architecture*, 14th International Architecture Exhibition La Biennale di Venezia

9. Bernhard Fuller, 'La pelle dell'edificio storico. Valori patrimoniali e tecnici della prassi del restauro dell'involucro,' in *Riuso del patrimonio architettonico*, by Bruno Reichlin and Bruno Pedretti (eds.), Silvana Editoriale, Mendrisio 2011, pp. 45-53.

10. Spartaco Paris, Michele Beccu, *L'involucro architettonico contemporaneo tra linguaggio e costruzione / Contemporary architectonic envelope, between language and construction*, RDesign Press, Rome 2008.

11. Kent Kleinman and Leslie Van Duzer, Mies van der Rohe. The Krefeld Villas '*MIes*', Princeton, Architectural Press, New York, 2005 p. 90. Also: Kenneth Frampton, 'Mies van der Rohe: Avant-Garde and Continuity', *Studies in Tectonic Culture*, 3, Rice University, Houston 1985. See also Werner Blaser, *Mies van der Rohe: The Art of Structure* (New York: Praeger, 1965), 21–23.

12. Francesca Picchi (ed.), *Prouvé inventore: 32 Brevetti. Prouvé, the inventor: 32 Patents*, in Domus 807, 1998, pp. 52-66.

13. Spartaco Paris, 'Jean Prouvé e l'esperienza dell'architettura come prodotto industriale', in M. Perriccioli (ed.), *Pensiero tecnico e cultura del progetto. Riflessioni sulla ricerca tecnologica in architettura*, Franco Angeli, Milano 2017, pp. 185-198.

Figure 20a / 20b.
Architectural envelope: the 'thickness' of surfaces.
The air space in the "doubleskin" facade of the Agbar Tower,
Design by Jean Nouvel, Barcelona

Figure 21.
Architectural envelope: the thickness of surfaces.
Elbphilharmonie Hamburg, Germany, Design by Herzog&deMeuron, 2001-2016.
Multifunctional double glazing curved:
Façade Josef Gartner GmbH, Detail of the the curved glass elements of the façade.

Figure 22.
Architectural envelope: The façade as inhabited space.
Transformation de 530 logements, bâtiments G, H, I, quartier du Grand Parc;
Design by Lacaton & Vassal, Druot, Hutin, Transformation of 530 dwellings, 2016.

Figure 23a / 23b.
Architectural envelope: The building skin and its fragile consistency.
Detail of the workshop building of the Bauhaus by Walter Gropius, 1925-26, Dessau.
Restoration project: Arge Bauhaus Brambach+Ebert Architekten Halle/Saale Pfister Schiess
Tropeano&Partner Architekten AG Zürich, 1998-2006

Figure 24.
Fenestration.
New Masters' Houses, Dessau, Germany,
Design by Bruno Fioretti Marquez 2010 -2014

Figure 25.
Fenestration.
Facade of Phillips Exeter Academy Library, Exeter, New Hampshire,
Design by Louis I. Kahn, 1967- 1972.

Figure 26.
Frames.
Grassi Museum of Applied Arts, Leipzig, Detail of glass frame,
Design by Joseph Albers, 1926

Figure 27.
Frames.
Fuel station prototype for 'Total', 1969,
Restoration as Info Tourism Office, Nantes, 2019
Design by Jean Prouvé.

Permeable fence

Bronzing structural steel frame.
Glass panel.
Opening type transom

B
G
C

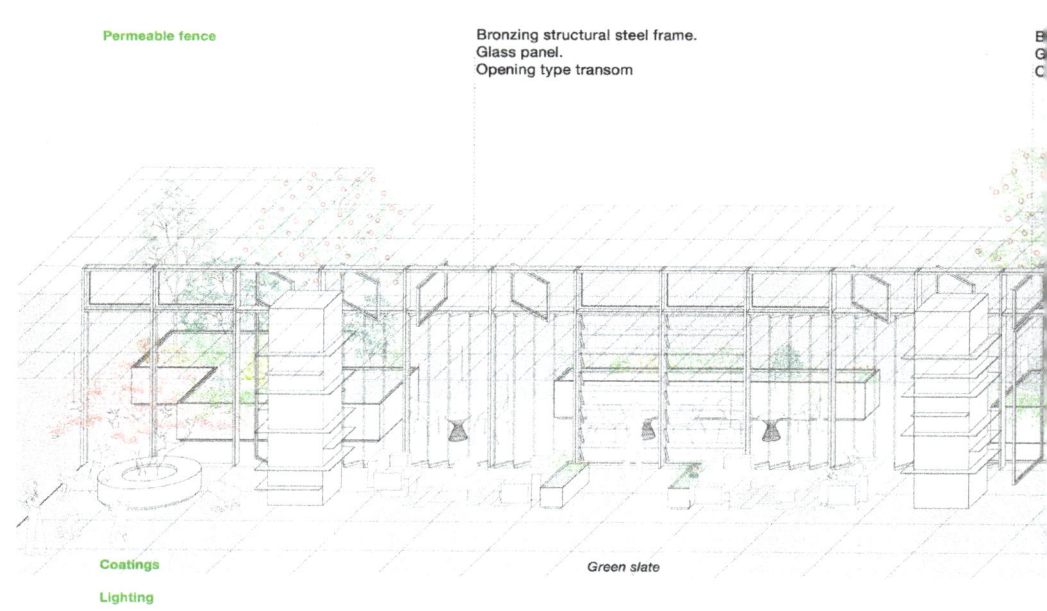

Coatings

Green slate

Lighting

Furnitures and
complements

Interior furniture:
Lago Modular Divano Air Sofa ,
upholstery Eco leather in warm
colours Col. 15 and Col, 24 in
Catalogue

Outdoor furniture:
Outdoor Lounge chair Collection
Heaven, in woven steel frame
Emu italia
Outdoor Coffee Table Collection
Heaven, in woven steel frame
Emu italia

Wooden platforms   Green slate

Outdoor lighting systems TAKE 10.11.
Light Source Suggested E27 ECO
Fluo max 1x23W

Outdoor furniture:
Outdoor Sofà Collection Ivy, in
woven steel frame Emu Italia
Outdoor Lounge chair Collection
Heaven, in woven steel frame
Emu Italia

Figure 28.
Abacus of design and architectural elements, furniture, lightings, complements, greenery.
Hanging Gardens, 2016 Chongqing South Bank Residential-skyscraper Green Eco Space.
International Design Competition,
Design by Spartaco Paris, Roberto Bianchi.

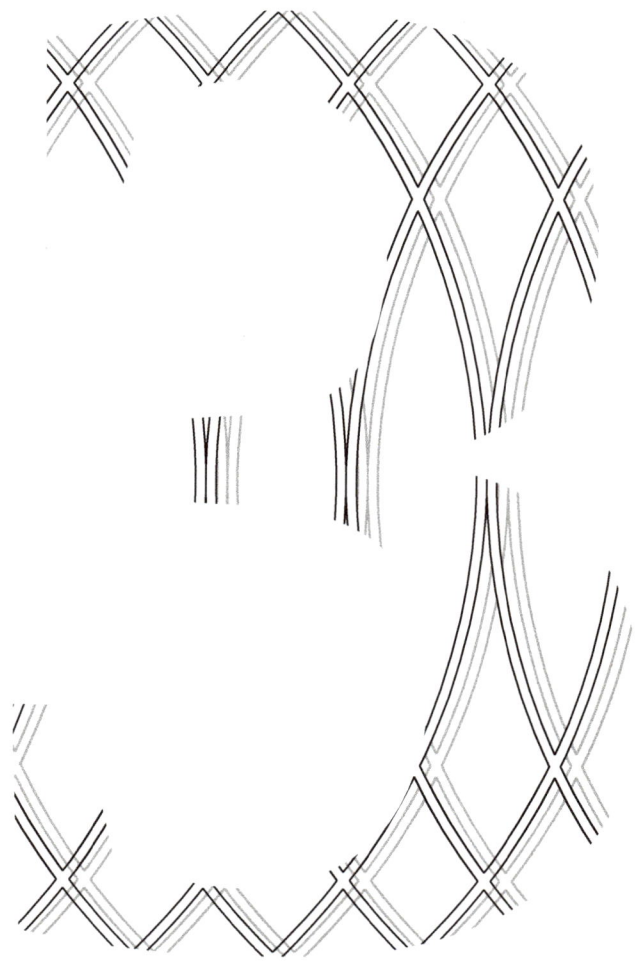

PART II
HOME
CHAPTER 3
FINISHES

3.1 On the surface of things

'I believe that the interior world deploys like a project: it can be mapped out and given form in terms of the architecture of stratification [...] In other words, film, architecture and clothing find a common point here as they 'stratify' on the surface of things. All three have the ability to shape a surface landscape that acts as a casing. They are our second skin, our sensory suit. They communicate our inner configuration and are the site of the dynamics of emotions.'

(Bruno, 2014)[14]

In architectural elements, the surface is the liminal layer, the place where all aspects of perception are concentrated, establishing a network of relationships with the beholder.

Of these aspects, the finish or 'face' establishes the quickest and most direct relationship with humans and their habitat, both on the outside and, especially, on the inside of architecture.

If we take the index of any historic architecture manual that originates in our western polytechnic culture, such as the one by Daniele Donghi[15], interior finishes are listed as soft-structure rather than hard-structure elements: components with a limited durability (between 10 and 25 years) compared to that of the building in which they are applied. Expected to be flexible and replaced several times during the life cycle of the outer shell, they are movable partitions, fittings, surface finishes, coverings and fixtures.

Within our habitat, finishes (in a broad sense) are used to ensure our visual, functional and climatic well-being. As with other products, in recent years we have witnessed a semantic extension of the role played by these elements. They now tend to establish a multi-sensorial and no longer exclusively visual relationship with us. This is possible thanks to the technological development of materials and production systems that offer increasingly sophisticated solutions to human needs, desires and emotions.

We seem to be witnessing the growing primacy of perception - in design as well as contemporary architecture. New surfaces have sensory and emotive characteristics that are enhanced by all available technology, becoming prominent design issues. We have photosensitive and three-dimensional types of wallpaper; textured reconstituted wood (see Concept Wood, produced by Alpi); and thermochromic types of concrete (see Solid Poetry by Droog Design) - just to mention a few examples of surfaces that give us unusual sensorial synaesthesiae[16], meaning that they solicit new ways of perceiving and experiencing reality by means of simultaneous and overlapping stimuli.

As Jonathan Franzen says:

'To speak more generally, the ultimate goal of technology, the telos of techne, is to replace a natural world that's indifferent to our wishes - a world of hurricanes and hardships and breakable hearts, a world of resistance - with a world

so responsive to our wishes as to be, effectively, a mere extension of the self'[17]

This is similar to what is happening today with interior finishes, where the consistency of surfaces is imbued with new experiences, removing physical and figurative weight from the material; where technological innovation is applied to coverings, making them smart materials that behave dynamically, unlike conventional building materials, which are static; where the emotional, comforting refuge has become our contemporary habitat, as we search for increasingly individual pleasure.

From: *Domus* n. 983 Settembre / September 2014. Finishes

3.2 Immersed in a new figuration

To use the term 'trappings', originally used to refer to harnesses and other accessories for horses, when we talk about architectural finishes may seem a little paradoxical, but it can instead help us to highlight the specific elements that have a decorative and representational function. Saddles, reins, sequins, ribbons, tassels, breastplates, plumes and decorations constitute a group of elements intended to cover, by displaying and concealing various parts of it, the body and structure of the horse.

Along with protection, decoration has always been one of the key elements when it comes to the representative function of architecture. Effectively, Adolf Loos already argued that the true architect always thinks in terms of skin as the element that conditions the way we inhabit a building.

Nowadays architectural finishes are defined through images and spaces that are increasingly distant from abstraction.

The recurring presence of naturalistic figures and references contributes to giving an expressive quality to contemporary buildings. We can see much evidence of this phenomenon if we wander around the pavilions at the Expo, where a certain experimentalism concerning forms and figures of natural or biophysical inspiration has become a simple tool to 'shock the bourgeoisie': we only need to think of the tree of life, the branches and/or stylised forests that cover box-like pavilions, and on to examples of simplified naturalistic intrusions.

In order to better understand the contours of this phenomenon, it is useful to make reference to the concept of empathy as defined by Wilhelm Worringer's theories on the psychology of style[18] from which the marketing strategies applied today to products for our surroundings amply draw on and which also regard the finishes of our interiors. The fast pace that is imposed on life today in fact requires formal solutions with a strong impact that are easy-to-use, whose 'aesthetic enjoyment' is immediate and not linked to slowly-developed contemplation. This is why the abstract approach, as opposed to an empathic one, occupies less space with respect to the latter and is relegated to interventions of minimalist conception or cases in which a tactile and perceptive characterization needs to be given to surface materials with designs based on transparency, reflection and sheen. The whole world of the image, especially that of digital animation, tends to offer hyper-realistic aesthetic simula-cra, expanded mimesis, altered nature: this is the world of visual stimuli in which we are immersed daily, a long way off from the abstract modernity that we were used to. This is why we are witnessing the extension of an infinite landscape - that refers back to images from the Arts and Crafts movement - of finishes and surfaces, today reproducible with the use of endless digital algorithms, that renew figurative repertoire in an explicit way, reinstating the impulse to imitate nature. The result is, however, a long way from art and not always interesting: tiles printed with leaves, arabesque decorations, naturalist and repeated patterns.

We return, with updated tools, to the field of applied arts, where a new virtuosity - technology - retrieves a bizarre value. What seems to newly prevail is an idolatry of the technical dimension of 'know-how' (*können*) rather than the artistic intention (*wollen*).

From: *Domus* n. 995 Ottobre / October 2015. Finishes

3.3. Techniques and the primacy of decoration

Over the course of recent years, many investigations into design have pointed to a certain predominance of decoration over spatial form when it comes to our con-temporary habitat. In the words of Riegl, today we are seeing the creation of the 'boundaries of space' prevail over the creation of space itself. In this dialectic, the role of surfaces and design experiments regarding their countless possible charac-teristics are hot topics, regarding not only the specific scale of interior architecture and furniture but also affecting the relationships between buildings and urban space.

Decoration has assumed new and original values that can contribute to pushing the boundaries of architecture-image, set by the productivist development of architec-ture as marketing.

Among the various studies, recent research by Rossana Carullo and Rosa Paglia-rulo[19] uses a kind of open taxonomy to investigate design actions on textile surfaces, defining a number of categories of conformation of a 'thickness' of material that, despite being small in size, is loaded with formal and technical content to the same extent as those of the building.

The actions of folding, stitching, weaving, layering of 'textile' design are altogether similar to the design operations on the 'thickness' of architecture, as an articulated assembly of planes and lines.

The reference is a 'highly authoritative' one, to Semper and the tectonics of textile surfaces, to the 'technical' modes of assembly and formation, that are able to de-termine aesthetic and expressive characteristics, specific to a new 'art of building'.

The role of decoration in our contemporary habitat thus acquires an increasingly important symbolic value, extending the sensory stimuli of the actual surface be-yond mere two-dimensionality.

Techniques typical of the 'decorative arts' have been retrieved and updated through research into materials and production methods: think of the 'drapery' that reappears in seemingly technical elements such as acoustic insulation panels, or the decorative patterns that use digital processes to update the stylised naturalistic motifs of 'classic' decorative wallpaper.

Research into the production of materials and forming methods, even in reduced thicknesses, has enabled the creation of moulded or engraved work reinstating the value of relief and *chiaroscuro*.

The return to the figuration of decorative elements finds in the production context the technological conditions for its renewal. Decorative patterns and stencils are generated by special processing programmes, that constitute easy-to-use digital tools that integrate with machines for the production and 'moulding' of products and today contribute to the definition of an expressive digital horizon, based on a multiplicity of repetition and seriality.

The most fascinating product solutions are those which reveal a cultural reinterpretation of the Arts and Crafts movement, where digital production tools continue to focus on the way things are made and not the formal outcome as such.

From *Domus* n. 998 Gennaio / January 2016. Interior decoration

3.4 Complementary furnishings as more than completing

Grammatically speaking, an adverbial phrase is a group of words that has the syntactic function of modifying and, in a certain sense, 'complementing' or completing a sentence. As distinct from the subject or object, such adverbials give sentences extra meaning, and without them language would be like a bare room without furniture. When it comes to interior design, then, complementary furnishings have a kind of syntactic function that is comparable to these adverbial word groups - modifying, completing and lending richer meaning to the living spaces in which they are inserted. Design has progressively attributed a broader function to these complementary furnishings, practically absorbing them into all the other 'grammatical' elements that surround them in space, almost becoming the sentence itself. Indeed, today the capacity to bring quality to living spaces is increasingly assigned to elements and objects of interior design, rather than to the form or character of the spaces themselves. In an analogy with architecture, it follows that the grammatical subject can be equated to space and habitation. The Belgian furniture designer Maarten Van Severen described his work (in *Domus* n. 764, October 1994) by comparing it to a painting by Pieter Saenredam, which portrays the nave of a church in relation to the furnishings: the divine scale and the human scale; structure and sub-structure. The complementary furnishings 'dwell' in the space like humans, constituting elements on a human scale, in a hierarchy of 'subjection' to the architecture. They thus establish an unavoidable, almost metaphysical relationship with living spaces.

In recent years, interior furnishings have increasingly taken centre stage, subverting the original hierarchy with the spaces that contain them. How? By favouring the interaction between surface and man-the consumer over the relationship with living space.

The domain of complementary furnishings is now expanding via categories of surfaces and the sense of pleasure. Both indulge today's trend for individual narcissism, which attributes meanings and desires to objects that go beyond the merely functional and/or representative sphere. Like the naturalist figures of the medieval exempla, or anecdotes, objects today solicit more persuasion than representation, through a simultaneous and instantaneous collection of stimuli that extend and amplify modes of interaction between man and artifact.

In expressive terms, there is accordingly an appeal to naturalism and a new figurativeness, couched within a renewed decorative approach that, consciously or otherwise, echoes and references the Arts and Crafts movement. This trend is heightened by the use of textures, patterns and the reiteration of figurative elements, made more accessible with digital methods and production systems. These expressive forms are more immediately recognisable than abstract forms, and they are more readily 'pleasing' and seductive due to their express aim of being desirable. Surface thus establishes a relationship of sensorial interaction with man, appealing not only to our eyes but also rediscovering touch as a sense that engenders a new physical pleasure in the relationship with objects. Sinuosity, softness, roughness and smoothness are tactile qualities at the centre of a specific exploration and design approach regarding the form of objects.

Complementary furnishings therefore expand their function within the sensory sphere, surpassing their original role of completing the space in which they are contained. They no longer limit themselves to absolving the multiple functions of living (sitting, working, preparing, relaxing, playing, sleeping, resting, containing, dividing, and nowadays also working and 'surfing'), but are there to seduce and console.

From: *Domus* n. 976 Gennaio / January 2014. Complements

3.5 Colours, design and the surface of things: combining interaction, techniques, education

'This way of searching will lead from a visual realisation of the interaction between colour and colour to an awareness of the interdependence of colour with form and placement [...]'

Josef Albers, *Interaction of Color*, Yale University Press, New Haven 1963

A vast amount of literature and numerous handbooks have been dedicated to the use of colour in design and architecture. Still among the most masterly are the teachings of Johannes Itten[20] and his pupil, the painter Josef Albers[21], who was first a student and then a lecturer at the Staatliches Bauhaus, before going on to establish a long teaching career in design in the United States .

The search for interaction between user and product - through the union of an abstract code and a tangible material, colour - is the central theme of Albers's work, as both an artist and a teacher.

It should be acknowledged that these early modern pedagogic experiences succeeded in linking the 'syntax' of colour with the psychology of perception, anticipating contemporary issues such as interaction, empathy, skin, surfaces, complex and precise modes of multi-sensorial relationships between man and artifact, between body and artwork, that have gone on to condition the products of today's living spaces.

These experiences have over time been further validated through the views of others in the field of basic design such as Bruno Munari, Tomás Maldonado and Giovanni Anceschi. Material culture itself, as Munari wrote in the preface to the Italian edition of Albers's *Interaction of Color*, is based on specific and consolidated mechanisms of colour perception, so for example the reds used in rural dwellings may be indirect complementary responses to the farmers' habit and physiological saturation of seeing green fields.

The 'return' to a new figuration - of easier empathy - was the subject of Tomás Maldonado's studies[22], observing a new, disruptive dominion of figurative representation and visual perception on abstraction, partly explaining it based on the role of digital technology.

A new emphasis on empathy towards sensory stimuli has taken design research in the direction of examining the surfaces of things. In his design courses, Albers defines them 'the skins of materials'[23].

These interfaces - in which are concentrated all the sensory implications of objects - determine, together with form, the sense of pleasure, a value that today seems to be prevalent in the multitude of objects among which we move and live. The use of colour seems to be the device - with its precise rules of composition - used to determine immediate interactions between human and artifact. This is the context in which we find the reasons for a renewed presence of colour in objects as a visual solution that has a more immediate and persuasive impact on users. This choice does not always correspond to a significance destined to last, but rather to pass quickly by, like fashion.

From: *Domus* n. 1001 Aprile / April 2016. Colour

Notes

14. Giuliana Bruno, *Surface. Matter of aesthetics, materiality and media*, University of Chicago Press, Chicago 2014, p. 18.

15. Daniele Donghi, *Manuale dell'architetto*, UTET, Torino1923.

16. Barbara Del Curto, Eleonora Fiorani, Caterina Passaro, *La pelle del Design. Progettare la sensorialità*, Lupetti, Milano 2010.

17. Jonathan Franzen's Commencement Speech at Kenyon College, May 2011

18. Wilhelm Worringer, *ibidem*.

19. Rossana Carullo, Rosa Pagliarulo, *Actions on surfaces. Softness*, Rubbettino, 2013.

20. Johannes Itten, *The Art of Color*, 1974. (Original title: *Kunst der Farbe*, Ravensburg, 1961).

21. Bruno Munari, Introduzione, in Albers, J. *Interazione del colore. Esercizi per imparare a vedere*. Milano. Il Saggiatore, 2005, pp. 8-9,

22. Tomas Maldonado, 'Arte e Artefatti'. Interview by Hans Urlich Obrist, Feltrinelli, 2010, *Figurazione e nuove tecnologie, pp. 23-27.*

23. Josef Albers, *Insegnare il Design / Teaching design* (*Werklicher Formunterricht*, in 'Bauhaus', nn. 2-3, 1928, pp. 3-7), in Marco Pierini (ed.), *Josef Albers*, Silvana Editoriale, Milano 2011, p. 92.

Figure 29.
On the surface of things. Detail of the Carnival rug, designed by the British
designer Paul Smith for The Rug Company, 2015

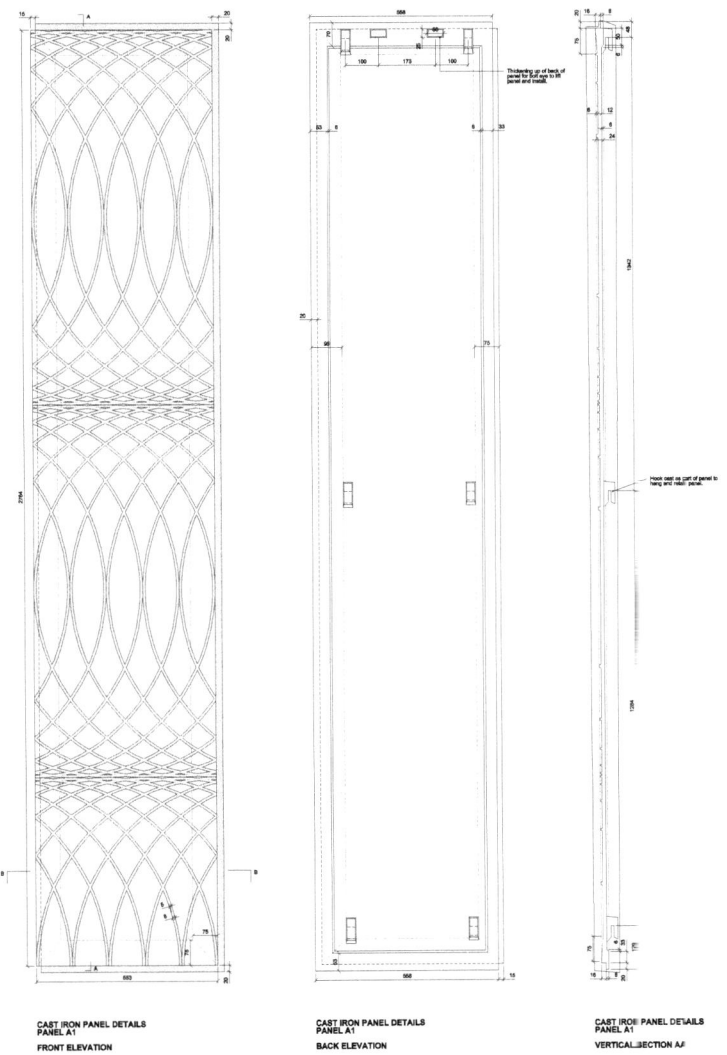

CAST IRON PANEL DETAILS
PANEL A1

FRONT ELEVATION

CAST IRON PANEL DETAILS
PANEL A1

BACK ELEVATION

CAST IRON PANEL DETAILS
PANEL A1

VERTICAL SECTION AA

Figure 30a / 30b.
Detail of iron cast element of facade,
No.11 Albemarle Street, Paul Smith London flagship,
designers: 6a architects London, 2013

Figure 31.
Immersed in a new figuration.
Solid poetry by Susanne Happle & Frederik Molenschot
in collaboration with Terratorium, 2018

Figure 32.
Techniques and the primacy of decoration.
Mouldings, A Store for Aesop, 2012 Totems II, Ornament & Crime, 2014

Figure 33.
Complementary furnishings as more than completing.
"Maarten Van Severen. Addicted to every possibility",
Installation Design by OMA.
Chairs: LC95A, CHL95, F88, Table: T88A

Figure 34.
Colours, design and the surface of things: combining interaction, techniques, education.
Nesting Tables, Design by Joseph Albers, 1926/1927; Wood, painted glass.
Table (white): 62,8 x 59,5 x 40 cm; table (yellow): 55 x 54 x 40 cm;
table (red): 47,5 x 48 x 40 cm; table (blue): 40 x 42 x 40 cm,
Josef & Anni Albers Foundation, Bethany US

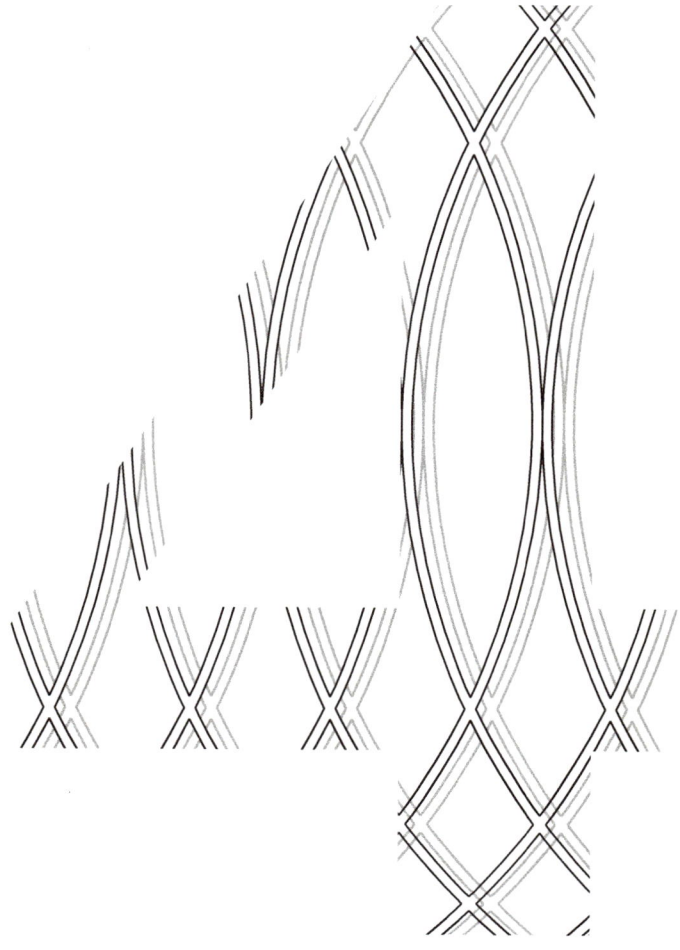

PART II
HOME
CHAPTER 4
FURNITURE

4.1 Furniture Design: machines and art

'…However, these items of furniture have an extraordinary, rather wicked power. Their impassive nature is a reckless, absolute dream but also denotes a state of anxiety, to design a chair once and for all in its content, meaning, lifeblood and form, so that all daily actions acquire meaning in that they are the repetition and reflection of that consistent pattern…

They indicate underlying contradiction and distress, the desire to reveal and disclose an order in production, that prices should be low, that they should be available to everyone; when instead they are irregular, extraordinary, out-of-the-ordinary and transgressive.' [24]

Reflecting on furniture from the rationalist era, in 1980, just 50 years on from that experience, Gae Aulenti analysed the expectations in terms of meaning that these objects had in creating a new, modern society, and how such hopes ran aground. However, the utopian content of these objects has remained so strong as to establish a continuous line in furniture production.

'Machine or art, in other words a device for the transformation of social energy in terms of production and distribution or antagonistic exchange,' [25] modern items of furniture are loaded with symbolic and representative content, increasingly forming a panorama that offers the hope and illusion of wellbeing, going beyond the role of providing 'decoration for the new house' [26].

The almost palingenetic function that design offers us today - even when limited to the sphere of furniture - is extraordinary.

In that part of the world where design is undergoing a process of modernisation, it is reproposing a model of modernity that has become outdated in the West. Here one thinks of the recent phenomenon of re-editions, where the best, modern, iconic designs reappear with minor updates enabling the revival of product ranges that were innovative 50 or 80 years ago. The *'machines à habiter'* from the last century have become modern classics, elevated to the level of archetypes to produce simplified or similar products for global distribution. Think of the many replicas of Mies's Barcelona chair, now a consumer product available at low prices in department stores worldwide.

'Machine or art.' The second modern trajectory for furniture design is that of the object verging on art and can be seen in the growing phenomenon of limited editions. Not without reason this phenomenon is being developed in the European context during a phase of economic contradiction in which luxury products have demonstrated a continual hold: promoting goods to the status of artworks is a way of elevating the one-off (or limited edition) artisan product. We also encounter a second new genre of designer furniture which goes back to being a special or rare artifact, rediscovering craft in the digital era, and satisfying the desire for a unique habitat. It corresponds to the undying demand for necessary luxury[27] in the first development of Italian industrial design. Furniture therefore remains a catalyst at the two extremes of contemporary design, divided between ever-modern industrial product, mass-produced on a global scale, and the rarity of a new, technologically advanced applied art.

From: *Domus* n. 979 Aprile / April 2014. Furniture

4.2 Furniture Design is not Fast-Fashion

If it is true what those in the trade say - that most pieces of designer furniture sold across the world were designed over 25 years ago - we can make a number of considerations. First of all, we should ask ourselves why products made in Italy are so successful. Certainly, one of the reasons lies in the capacity to produce objects endowed with a durable or 'slow' aesthetic able to stand up to changing trends and fashions. This has led to an ever-growing number of re-editions.

For some years now, legendary furniture brands have been investing considerable resources in updated productions of pieces designed and made in the era that spans from the post-war years to the end of the 1970s, whose manufacture was interrupted or suspended for some reason.

The phenomenon of making re-editions of the classics of modern design underwent a renewed impulse about ten years ago with events and cultural manifestations such as the Triennale Design Museum presenting icons of Italian design.

The intrinsic value in terms of material and use of these 'icon-objects' has acquired an additional symbolic value linked to image, communication and recognisability, similar to what happens with literary classics.

In a newspaper article Italo Calvino wrote, 'the classics are books that exert particular influence both when they impose themselves as unforgettable and when they hide in the folds of memory, camouflaging themselves in the collective or individual subconscious.'[28]

Among the illustrious design classics reissued in 2008 by Cassina for its collection '*I Maestri*' was the celebrated Luisa chair designed by Franco Albini in the late 1930s, manufactured at five different times, with the longest period of production being by Poggi, who sold it from 1955 to 1980. The popularity of re-editions has had an effect not only on the market, but also on production: many companies like to rest on their laurels by coasting along on the iconic quality of certain products. They invest more in old successes than in the new and experimental. The production of re-editions has implications for industrial production and craftsmanship. An object produced today cannot be a perfect replica of the original due to changed methods and technologies, but an iconic appearance is not easily undermined by the substitution of elements or joints or the use of wood instead of metal - see the abovementioned Luisa or Cicognino.

The relocation of historic pieces to our times also involves a variation in surface attributes: new fabrics and colours can accommodate changes of taste and update a product in response to the logics of the market and the spirit of the times.

From: *Domus* n. 981 Luglio / Agosto 2014. Furniture

4.3 …There was a time when furniture came from… cars

There was a time in the history of design, which nowadays seems like ancient history, when new ideas for furniture were inspired by forms and technology borrowed from distant worlds such as the automobile, aeronautics, or other manufacturing industries. During a period when modern Italian design was still in its early stages, which might now seem like a distant archaeological past, technological transfers from manufacturing sectors, other than those specific to furniture-making, brought opportunities for experimentation and profound innovation, as well as contributing to determining the reasons for the success of many designers and of Italian furniture.

Think of the forays made by Marco Zanuso into the world of car design and construction and his explorations into innovative new concepts and forms - for example the monocoque chassis, or single-body, shell-like structure - that he was able to transfer into the world of furniture. Think of the now legendary Lambda chair produced by Dino Gavina (1959-64) and presented as three overlapping orthogonal projections, a method 'imported' from the world of car bodywork[29] .

Or we can look to the world of aeronautics for certain types of cladding or sheet steel: metal doors bent and riveted like aeroplane wings in the designs of Jean Prouvé and other pioneers of a heteronomous modernity whose language is programmatically open to cross-pollination from other fields.

Or another of Zanuso's ideas, that of bringing a material employed for military purposes - in this case foam rubber - to the world of furniture, through the legendary experience of Arflex.

These are innovations based on a transfer - not always a conscious one, but one that becomes an opportunity to create new forms - of technologies and tools from one manufacturing industry to another.

At present, the most innovative and potentially fertile branch of technology seems to be 3D printing, which also puts a potential army of designers in a position to become manufacturers of their own products. It seems, however, that this technological development has yet to bring about consolidated innovations in terms of form and above all production.

Furniture manufacturing is organised into its own specific systems and as many[30] have observed, we are at a stage in which what seems more interesting is the potential of an impetus towards a new diffusion of craft rather than the forms that may result from it.

In effect, if we consider the finest workmanship from pre-industrial times, it was the teaching of technical knowledge that determined the actual formal qualities of consolidated languages. No technological innovation has in a short space of time been able to produce formal innovations that have then been translated into lasting and established forms, while the latter have instead needed a longer time to be transformed into forms that belong to a new technique. At present what seems more relevant are these new 3D printing systems and their capacity to produce copies rather than their ability to build interesting physical forms.

Instead, we see fertile ground for new inventions in updating and re-designing products, in terms of style and production, that have become classics and have entered the figurative imagination of the public[31] .

From: 2015 *Domus* n. 990 Aprile / April 2015. Furniture

4.4 Variable and invariable forms of furniture: tables

Amid the grand array of shapes and forms that inhabit our spaces today, where originality and novelty are the order of the day so as to be sure to attract attention, arouse curiosity and satisfy the desires of consumers, furniture has been transformed, and traditional product categories redefined, for a market that is increasingly demanding and discerning. If it is true, as Stefano Giovannoni observed, that a designer product costs to the public on average five times more than an 'ordinary' product, it is inevitable that characteristics such as being unique or iconic elevate the object to status symbol or accessible form of art. The possibilities offered by manufacturing technology, which is able to provide increasingly personalised responses to individual desires and the trend for originality, have meant that many product types now elude univocal classification, instead they often create new inventions or combine one thing with another: nomad beds that become totems, bookcase-walls, tent-beds or storage beds or pouffes-cum-domestic appliances.

In products that are more morphologically stable in their evolution and transformation - like chairs - variation in style is provided by materials, ergonomics, finishes, colours and the relationship with the human body.

Meanwhile, an increase in the number of collectors of designer-objects has determined the permanence in the market of some products that, all the while undergoing modification in a seemingly imperceptible way, have remained constant in terms of production. Think of the Less table by Jean Nouvel, conceived and produced by Unifor in 1994 for the offices at the Fondation Cartier: twenty years on, this table has been subjected to continuous manufacturing refinements that can be seen in its improved performance and the quality of the finishing materials.

Of all types of furniture, in its process of transformation the table is certainly the most stable and permanent. Firstly because it is an object whose form is intrinsically linked to its function. What is more, the table interacts with the very notion of space. It is shelter and support, it can always be reduced to its basic elements - a horizontal surface and supports - that make up the structural elements[32]. It is no coincidence that the terms 'table' and 'trestle' have been mutated from architecture to define primary structural arrangements. Marc Dubois[33] observed that over the course of design history, the table has evolved more as a reinterpretation of the archetype, or previous models, than in terms of actual morphological reinventions, even when technological innovation has brought about more significant changes. The level of permanence in the style of tables within the sphere of interior design is particularly evident, so much so that tables are less present (at least numerically) in collections, exhibitions and publications on furniture, which have always concentrated more on sofas, chairs, lamps and objects that are less restricted and therefore more likely over time to undergo changes in design. This permanence allows us to recognise tables as being primary structures of architecture, as elements that lie at the origins of furniture but not necessarily as being original.

From: *Domus* n. 993 Luglio–Agosto / July–August 2015. Furniture

4.5 The details aren't details. They make the product. The connections, the connections, the connections

Nowadays, the term 'connections' is perhaps linked more to the immaterial sphere of interpersonal relationships than it is to its material origins as any manner of ways to link materials and elements together. In the four arts as defined by Semper – textiles, ceramics, tectonics-carpentry and stereotomy – the question of connections has always been the original root of the detail, in other words, the design technique or art used to bind, fasten, tie or join the parts and elements of a system. From applied arts to industrial design, it is still the physical and semantic way to identify the qualities of products that belong to the world of design. On the scale of a piece of furniture, it is one of the most significant elements of design, in which the very origin of the modern piece of furniture can be identified as an assembly of parts or a moulded piece. In the first instance, as confirmed by the latest design research, connections continue to have their own specific structure in their joints. This is indeed what often expresses the beauty of a piece of furniture: the way the different materials are emphasised, the form of the legs of a chair or a sofa, the way the supporting structure is connected to the main elements, the fixings, the stitching, the folds, the mechanisms of the moving parts. In this context, the role of technology is highly significant: furniture is much more sophisticated when the 'connections' or the mechanisms for moving, rotating and sliding the various parts are concealed from sight. Separating, detaching, overlaying, lining-up and juxtaposing are some of the ways the designer connects the various parts of a piece of furniture, composing a unity that we recognise as a product belonging to the field of design. In the second instance, when the processes of imagining and shaping furniture emerge through the moulding of forms, the connections tend to disappear.

In the first mode, technique helps to shape and define the language of the product, and in the second, prevailing over production tools and methods, is artistic expression.

The title of the famous essay by Ralph Caplan *Making Connections: The Work of Charles and Ray Eames*[34], written for an exhibition of the designers' work, highlights the core of the specific approach to design by the famous American designers as the art of resolving problems via connections. The concept of connection is, according to the Eames, intrinsic to design and architecture. 'Connections between what? Between such disparate materials as wood and steel, between seemingly alien disciplines such as physics and painting, between clowns and mathematical concepts, between people and architecture, mathematicians and poets, philosophers and corporate executives'[35]. Eames himself, wrote Caplan, believed that, 'the details aren't details. They make the product. The connections, the connections, the connections'[36].

The Eames' work on connections is still relevant today, setting an important precedent for designers such as Antonio Citterio who explicitly cited it as one of his references not only in terms of form but also as a general approach to designing furniture, during a conference held at the Sapienza University in Rome in 1997. The technological mechanism for forming joints and making them function is an integral part of the design and was one of the distinguishing features of the American approach to design compared to Europe's, whereas today it has been completely assimilated into design all over the world. Observing the distinguishing features of contemporary furniture, one cannot but notice how the theme of connections is still important and also helps to give a material basis to the intangible and figurative in the digital world.

From: *Domus* n. 1002 Maggio / May 2016. Furniture

Notes

24. Gae Aulenti, 'Una geometria mentale', in *Rassegna* n. 4, Il disegno del mobile razionale in Italia 1928/1948, Bologna, 1980, p. 15.

25. Gae Aulenti, *Ibidem*.

26. Edoardo Persico, 'Tendenze e realizzazioni', *La casa bella*, 29, May 1930, pp. 27-33.

27. Renato De Fusco, *Storia del design*, Laterza, Roma-Bari, 2007.

28. Italo Calvino, 'Italiani vi esorto ai classici', in *l'Espresso*, 20 June 1981 – ('Italians, I urge you to the classics').

29. Roberta Grignolo (ed.), *Marco Zanuso, Scritti sulle tecniche di produzione e di progetto*, Silvana Editoriale, Mendrisio, 2013.

30. Benedikt Huber, Jean-Claude Steinegger (eds.). *Jean Prouvé. Une architecture par l'industrie*. Architektur aus der Fabrik. Industrial Architecture, Les Editions d'Architecture, Les Éditions d'Architecture Artemis, Zurich, 1971.

31. Lorenzo Damiani, 'Questioni di Design/Design matters', in *Domus* n. 980, maggio/May 2014, pp. 102-103.

32. Spartaco Paris, 'A Table is like a Building. Archetipo di architettura', in *A design selection, Diid Disegno Industriale | Industrial Design* n. 56, p. 111, Rome 2013.

33. Marc Dubois, 'La dimensione del tavolo', in *Lotus International* n. 98, p. 112, Milan 1998.

34. Ralph Caplan, 'Making Connections: The Work of Charles and Ray Eames', in Connections: *The Work of Charles and Ray Eames*, catalogue of the exhibit curated by John and Marilyn Neuhart, which took place at the Fredrick Wight Art Gallery, University of California, Los Angeles, 7 December 1976 to 6 February 1977.

35. *Ibidem*.

36. *Ibidem*.

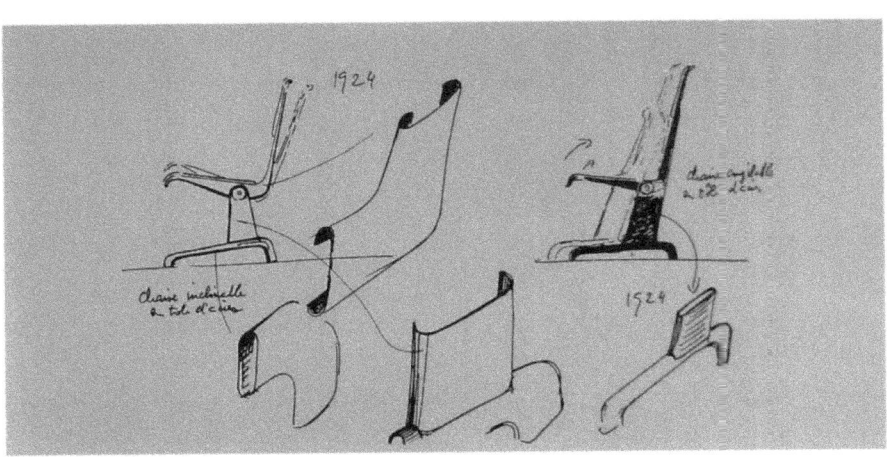

Figure 35.
Furniture Design: machines and art.
Frame and sketches of a stackable folding chair,
Design by Jean Prouvé, 1924-1920

Figure 36.
Furniture Design is not Fast-Fashion.
Modular bookstore LB7 – INFINITO – 1956/57, reedition Cassina 2008,
Design by Franco Albini

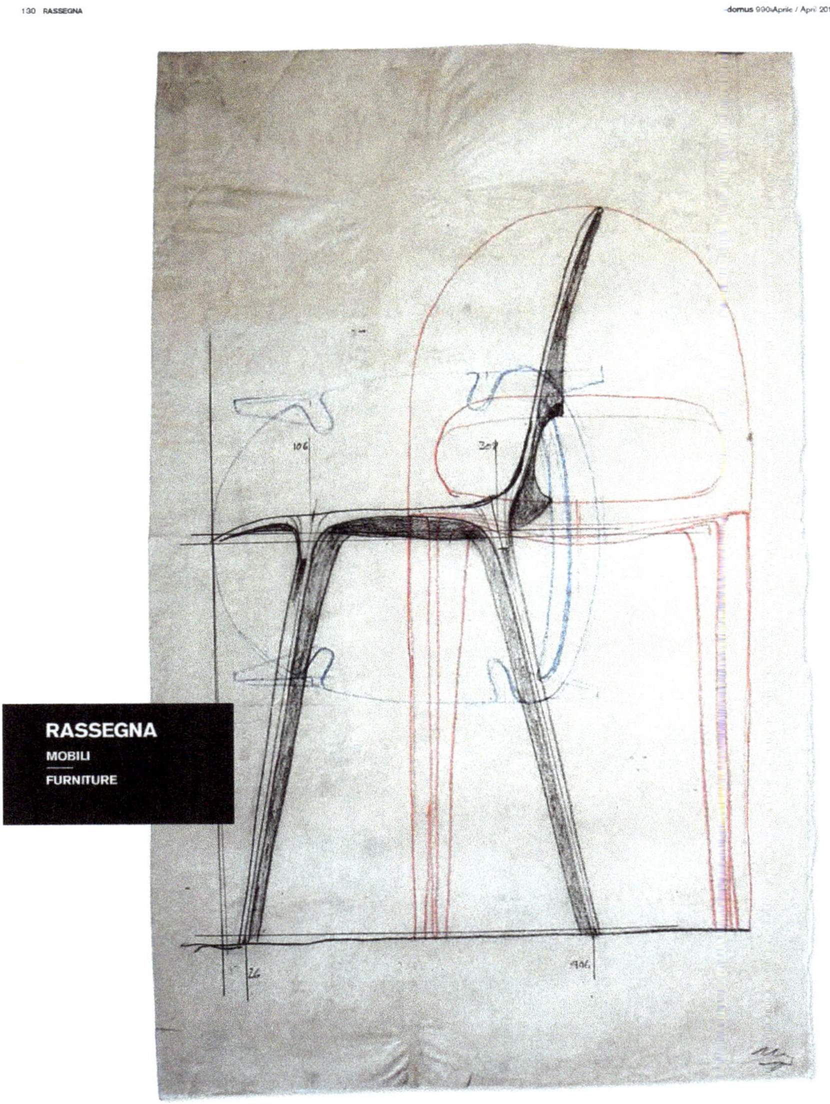

RASSEGNA
MOBILI
FURNITURE

Figure 37.
Technological transfer.
Borrowed from the world of the automobile, this preparatory sketch helped Marco Zanuso to define the
lines of the Lambda chair produced by Dino Gavina (1959-64).
Mendrisio, Archivio del Moderno, Fondo Marco Zanuso, D C2,
in Domus 990, April 2015. Rassegna Furniture

Figure 38.
Technological transfer.
From Furniture to automotive. Process of moulding of a sofa,
Design by Kevin Rice for Mazda, 2015

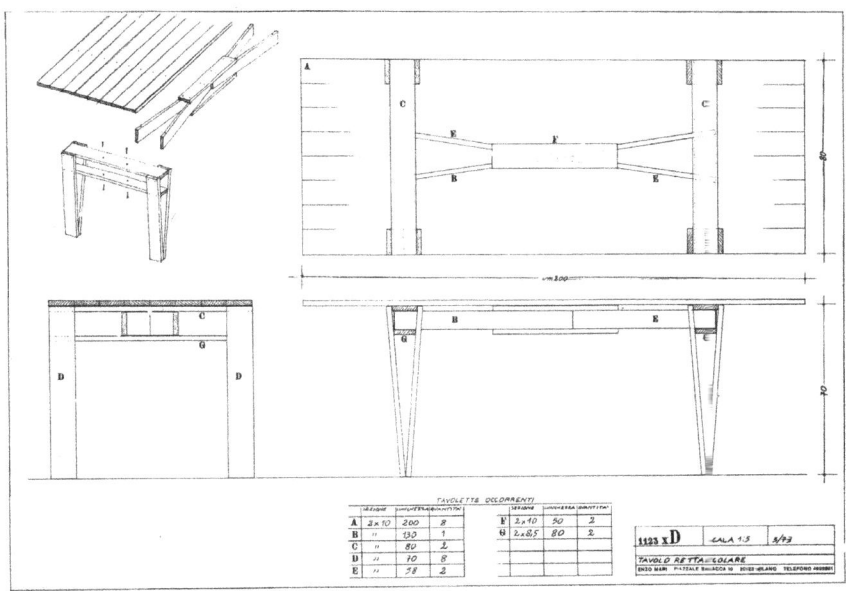

Figure 39.
Variable and invariable forms of furniture: Tables as primary structures.
1123XD. Tavolo Rettangolare,
Design by Enzo Mari, 1974

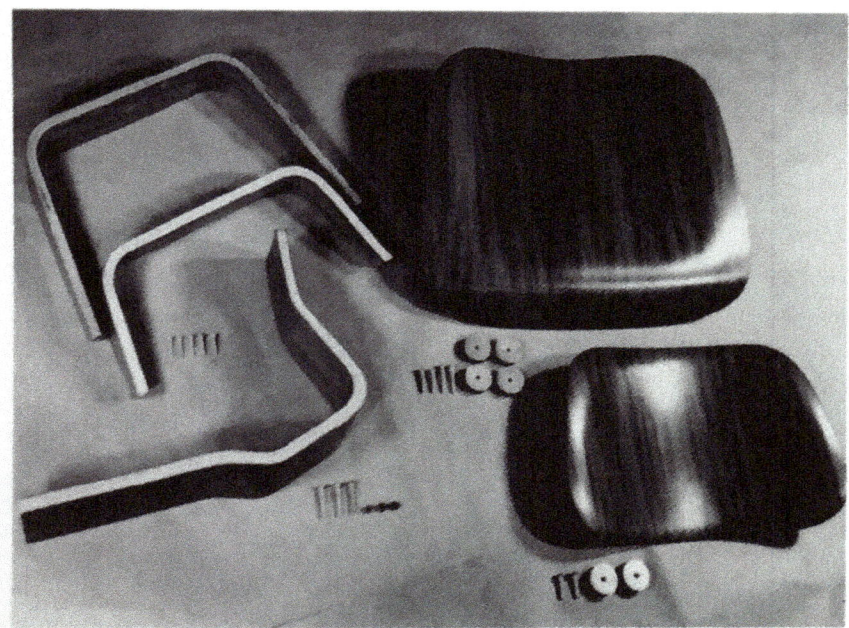

Chair parts before assembly

Plywood chair details.

Figure 40a.
"The details aren't details. They make the product."
The work of Charles and Ray Eames, by Ralph Caplan,
Cover of booklet; Plywood chair details; Chairs parts before assembly, 1941.

Figure 40b.
Ralph Caplan "The work of Charles and Ray Eames",
UCLA Art Council / Frederick S. Wright Art Gallery; December 7, 1976-February 6, 1977.

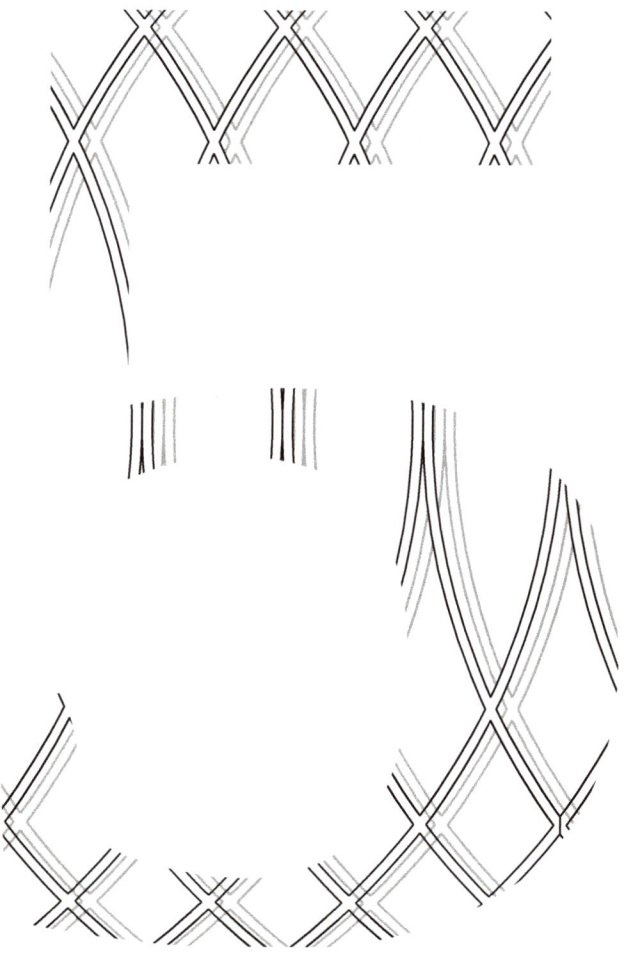

PART II
HOME
CHAPTER 5
TYPES OF SPACE

5.1 Kitchens: technological innovation and production; current trends.

Aside from the social implications that concern the way the contemporary environment has altered kitchen spaces and the way they are used, it is worth considering how and in what way the relationship between the conception and production of systems and components has changed in the contemporary kitchen. As with other sectors in the market, manufacturing has been progressively sensitized towards identifying strategies for reducing energy consumption, optimizing production cycles, selecting and developing the use of eco-compatible materials; generally adopting methods and strategies with the aim of considering sustainability not as a punitive imposition but as an opportunity to add value to products. With this in mind, kitchen manufacturers are adopting mainly materials and production technologies that use primary, 'secondary' or 'tertiary' materials in which the residue from sequences of cutting processes get smaller and smaller to the point of becoming particles and sawdust. These are then re-formed into panels and sheets of chipboard and MDF and, with the addition of glues, constitute the chief material used in the production of furniture. Changing needs regarding the purpose, size and use of our surroundings have also led to the integration of the kitchen into more convivial areas of the house, above all through exploring the form and finish of fittings and domestic appliances.

Observing technological innovation in manufacturing, a current trend that deserves consideration is that of minimising the amount of material necessary for the production of kitchen fittings, whether they are finishes - the use of nanotechnologies for coatings - or structural elements. Experimentations underway, that could soon become real innovations in products and systems, regard the use of 'framed' systems (using aluminium profiles) clad with thin panels that enable a notable reduction in material as well as recyclability - all in the spirit of sustainability in industrial production, offering new areas of research in the design and production of kitchens in the years to come. The analogy that comes to mind is that with the *maison domino* of the Modern Movement, in which the clear separation between structural components and infill components can be a renewed reference in the research and production of kitchen furniture for the coming years.

> *'Only when, on the one hand the demands of modern life, and on the other technical improvements, have determined a contraction and at the same time, a specification of spaces within the home, will the kitchen come to acquire a completely new look.'* [37]

Over the course of his entire design career, Marco Zanuso always took an interest in the poetics of technical objects; in 1945 he edited *La Cucina*, a book dedicated to this part of the house and its evolution, for the series *I Quaderni di Domus* directed by architects Lina Bo and Carlo Pagani.

Looking at the diffusion of the mass-produced kitchen in American society, Zanuso could not but highlight the differences and the passage towards modernity that the Italian home was undergoing during the process of reconstruction, represented in particular by the evolution of the kitchen. This space, and above all its technical appliances (for food preparation, washing and storing of dinnerware), are the elements that have undergone the most evident technological and formal transformations within the domestic environment.

Let us try and consider, aside from the recent and progressive inclusion of the kitchen within the convivial area of the home, the elements that have most been subjected to renewal, development and innovation. At the same time as Zanuso was writing, the production of fittings for kitchens - then limited to being rooms for food preparation - was still mostly carried out at an artisan level in Italy, whereas nowadays industrialised manufacturing offers a response to assorted and specific demands within the same widely-acknowledged standards.

As well as the development of manufacturing technologies that approach factory production with greater environmental awareness, the inclusion of the kitchen inside the house, intended as a living space and not only perceived in relation to its primary function, has resulted in two kinds of transformation and corresponding areas of research and design development.

On the one hand, optimisation of the ergonomic aspects has had an effect on the form and dimension of fittings and increased the depth of the worktop, resulting in the widespread adoption of islands and peninsular units.

On the other, the technical characteristics of products have altered in response to increasingly specific demands, dictated both by functional requirements and by growing standards linked to tactile and visual perception of the surface finishes of technical elements and fittings. This sphere has also lent itself to the transfer of innovative technologies originating from other fields of research, able to structure and reinterpret all manner of technical elements, from worktops to sinks, taps and cooker hoods - wall-mounted, disappearing, sculptural - right up to domestic appliances and devices for food preparation.

By importing and modifying elements from the professional working-kitchen, the contemporary kitchen has heavily influenced its solely technical function, with a number of domestic requisites mutated from living spaces in the home.

From: *Domus* n. 981 Giugno / June 2014 and from Domus n. 987 Gennaio / January 2015. Kitchens

5.2 Bathrooms: empathy and the evolution of production and technologies

The Baths of Diocletian, built between 298 and 306 AD, were the largest public baths in Rome, extending over 13 hectares. Up to 3,000 people could gather in these baths to pass the time and care for their bodies, transiting through the special sequence of rooms known as the *tepidarium, frigidarium* and *caldarium*, spaces that were later transformed by Michelangelo into the Basilica of St. Mary of the Angels. At the National Museum of Rome, founded in 1889, the imposing *Aula Decima* - a smaller space within the original building - today gives us an indication of the immensity of the complex.

Linked to the sphere of *otium*, or leisure, activities related to bodily care and hygiene were for a long time communal, arising from public and social interest in personal care. Hence a convivial dimension was introduced to this kind of human activity, as well as a need to define and create special architecture for this function.

Modern society, from its beginnings to the present day, has been increasingly centred on the individual, and as such this activity has become entirely personal. Included in housing from the post-war period, the domestic bathroom initially represented a symbol, similar to the myth of the washing machine and the refrigerator, that of aspired-for or achieved well-being. In recent years its role has been extended even further, going hand-in-hand with the contemporary individual's quest for pleasure, taking the design of fittings for this space into a totally new era. Over the last 30 years, this manufacturing sector has become increasingly significant, to the point of becoming a key sector of Italian industry, where a constant search for new looks and types of products is much in evidence, involving large numbers of designers.

Behind products and components that do not seem to have particularly evident technological content - such as sanitary fittings or taps - there lies major and often significant innovation in terms of manufacturing systems.

Such advancements often aim towards a more ethical and sustainable industry, where the technology is there but you don't necessarily see it, and it regards a multiplicity of aspects of the design and production process, from the conception of a product to its launch. Many leading Italian manufacturers in this sector - a significant example being in ceramics - have solidly adopted a system that increasingly designs for the whole life cycle of the product. Life Cycle Design (LCD) is a process-based approach that enables the most eco-sustainable options to be evaluated and selected during the entire production process, from conception to launch.

It should be underlined that this condition occurs through the integration of two specific aspects of the Italian industrial system, which are less evident compared to physical and aesthetic qualities, but no less significant: the updating of local - often craft-based - manufacturing traditions and technological innovation in order to optimize the use of raw materials and resources via automated production and the use of nanotechnology (for example for glazing sanitaryware). As such, it is a means of projecting the industry towards the future.

Aside from the evolution of the role of the bathroom within the domestic context - having become increasingly important when it comes to representing desired or achieved status - in these pages it is interesting to consider the relationship between the products themselves and the industrial strategies being adopted by this sector of the market. Bathroom products - I refer particularly to sanitary ware and finishes - have a close relationship with advanced technology and are intrinsically linked to the manufacturing strategies of the industry itself where, alongside well-established industrial values such as optimising efficiency, quality-control and the economics of production, there is now an increasing emphasis on the new shared values of eco-sustainability and energy-saving.

Although it may seem to the end-user that the products of the bathroom industry are not particularly high on technological content compared to other items - for example ICT products - in reality they conceal industrial strategies and technologies applied to the process and products that are both complex and innovative.

The leading companies in this sector are focused on a kind of 'preventative-design' approach for 'green' production, that offers the opportunity for more sensitive users/customers to choose products characterised not only by a discernible aesthetic content, but also by their high level of

environmental efficiency. This means that the whole of the supply-chain has to be able to monitor the consumption of material resources, heating and electrical energy as well as land-use throughout the entire lifecycle of the product, from its conception to its disposal.

As well as acrylic materials, it is on ceramic products - that would seem to be relatively low on technological content - that manufacturers are focusing their research, one that pays increasing attention to developing a more responsible approach to production, aided by the fact that ceramic is

already in itself a hygienic, hard-wearing, inexpensive and mouldable material.

Therefore, improving the quality of products and processes, in addition to considerably enhancing the quality of living as a whole, represents a possible contribution for a ceramic manufacturer who chooses the path of eco-sustainable development. Provided, of course, that he adjusts to the terms, modes and costs required by such a commitment. Whereas until twenty years ago this path was reserved to an elite, today (luckily, for us all) it has become a goal for that 'healthy' share of companies that have decided not to give in to the crisis, but to aim at a creative, technological and productive transformation instead, as a remedy for well-being and progress.

Life Cycle Design - which requires the planning of the following phases: pre-production, production, transportation, distribution and recycling - does not appear to be a smooth strategy to apply to the whole industry of ceramic fittings, at least not if entirely managed by a single company. As a matter of fact, the manufacturing of ceramic fittings - which boasts a century-long history - is, just like many other product categories, part of a supply chain that involves many actors: from raw materials (provided by extractive and chemical industries), to the integration of accessories (a role for metallurgical and furniture industries), to end-of-life re-cycling (although still in its embryonic stage and not yet systematized, mainly left in the hands of companies in charge of collecting construction waste).

Use of the Life Cycle Design approach makes it possible to study and reduce the environmental impact of products over the course of their entire life cycle: through all the phases of design, production, transport, distribution, recycling.

In the field of sanitary ware and ceramic products - as in other manufacturing sectors for more sophisticated components -, Life Cycle Design requires a high level of integration between all the parties in the supply chain: from the producers of raw materials (chemical and mining industry) to the workers and on to recycling at the end of its useful life, a sector today still largely at a developmental stage.

From the point of view of manufacturing technology, the main innovations for sustainability, as well as improved techniques for glazing, regard the evolution of robotized systems of casting at high-pressure that enable maximum optimisation.

This has determined not only better-quality products - through the optimisation of energy consumption and raw materials - but also an improvement in the conditions of the workers, an important factor for the establishment of a more ethical industry.

From: *Domus* n. 980 Maggio / May 2014, Domus n. 988 Febbraio / February 2015. Bathroom

5.3 Work spaces. From open space to home office. Technological innovation in office design

'The building is arranged around a vast central atrium that is used as a workspace, recreation hall or exhibition area, according to the occasion. The offices around it, accessed by gangways, are no longer the designated place for work, because every employee possesses a mobile phone.'

Jean Nouvel [39]

A bed has always remained more or less a bed, just like chairs and armchairs. They respond to dimensions and demands that may have been modified according to aesthetic and technological innovations, but always retain a kind of intrinsic primary form that is both recognisable and unchangeable.

In the case of offices however, the transformations that have taken place over the last 20 years have been much more profound and have had consequences on the typology of workspaces, the ways they are used, the tools, their forms and their size. The revolution in information and computing technology, energy savings (see the catchphrases of our times: 'sustainability' and 'smart' buildings or cities) and the recession are the three paradigms that have altered demands, needs, modes of working and ways of occupying the workplace, particularly the office. What effect have they had on the elements that conform and define office spaces, whether traditional, domestic, shared, nomadic or temporary? What has changed in the 3.0 era, the age of co-workers and home offices?

The notion itself of what constitutes an office has been transformed over time, from the early office buildings at the end of the 19th century to the present day. Since the modernist model of Taylorism, the standardised and totalitarian open-plan office has become a thing of the past. Environments dedicated to working have gradually acquired the need to be pleasant, convivial and domestic. While technological innovations in the fields of lighting and air-conditioning have overcome the restriction linked to building depth, changing demands and working conditions have contributed to a new definition of the features, spatial elements and fixtures that characterise the world of the office. On the one hand, workstations have followed the development of the principal instrument of work, from the typewriter to the laptop, reducing in depth from 70 to 60 centimetres over a relatively short time. This has then meant moving away from the concept of the traditional desk and has given leeway to economy of space. Where up until 15 years ago there were two workstations, today there might be three or four.

The resulting increase in proximity has in turn demanded a suitable response in terms of acoustic and visual comfort, bringing about new solutions that have gradually provided an increasing amount of privacy. What is more, current modes of working have led to workstations being configured differently, losing their traditional territorial nature (each with one personal workstation) and becoming spaces used in turn by numerous users in which the chairs and desks - exploiting increasingly sophisticated ergonomics - offer more and more options for customisation.

Finally, coexisting demands of shared space for some working activities, typical of open-plan spaces, and separation for others, like the traditional single-cell models, have brought about the development of new island-spaces for private meetings, their edges defined by fixed furniture, glazed walls and other devices.

From: *Domus* n. 984 Ottobre / October 2014. Office

5.4 The evolution of the work space: from the nternet of things to the new 'studiolo' or small studio

At the 2015 SaloneUfficio, a large installation entitled *The Walk. A different vision of the world of work* by Michele De Lucchi presented a picture of the heterogeneous and mutating landscape that is today's workspace, illustrating some of the transformations that are taking place. The workspace is being completely re-thought: offices are becoming creative environments, customised and with the same kind of appeal as 'nomadic' workplaces: homes, parks, stations and means of transport. The current trend is to make the office increasingly domestic and friendly but at the same time more transversal and interconnected.

The range of products currently on offer reflects the complex integration between the increasing demand for privacy and the need for shared activities, proximity and alternating users, who tend to move around workstations more and more. The contemporary workspace has been deeply influenced by a number of factors that lie behind this evolution: the transformation of the dimensions of workstations brought about by the evolution of ICT, modalities of shared work and the integration between individual and group work (see *Domus* n. 984, October 2014).

Pressing demands to multitask along with exposure to multiple stress from information and communication technologies cause us to feel a new desire for protection - acoustic and visual - that brings with it a need to define places suitable for concentration and 'islands' of individual well-being within modular and changeable archipelagos for work. Quite simply, one seeks in the office the concentration that in general we find in the study at home, or when we are wearing headphones. These are the preconditions that underlie the extensive range of new systems for partitioning and dividing spaces that we found at the Salone this year, all offering remarkable performance in terms of acoustics, acting as filters or visual separations. These are visible both on the scale of partition walls as well as on a much smaller one, as dividers between workstations.

This demand to find once more concentration and protection away from the multiple stresses to which we are subjected has led to the revival of the archetype of the 'studiolo', or private-study as a kind of 'return to the future', while on the other hand the Internet of things is bringing to fruition the passage towards a 'ubiquitous' society where the potential of the digital enables us to have all the information we require and contact with people wherever we are, on increasingly intelligent supports.

A case in point is the work table; take the famous Nomos designed by Foster almost 20 years ago: its top is now not just a support for objects but a 'smart', interactive dashboard, thereby making a transition to where the formal paradigms of modernity find reason to be and are updated as the digital era comes to a head/in line with the digital era.

From: *Domus* n. 991 Maggio / May 2015. Office

5.5 Outdoor space: open air spaces as public building

'Beauty doesn't stand for itself. Just like real beauty is tied to usefulness, urban planning design achieves the demand for beauty if it addresses the inherent needs of traffic, construction and sanitation' [40]

Traditionally, in schools of architecture, architectural design courses were - and still are for the most part - for teaching how to design a building, the solid part, the building mass, the 'positive'. The space outside the building was often left as a vague negative area that someone else (a landscape architect or town-planner) would design, specifying the forms and characteristics of the separate spaces and the kind of planting. Still today, here in Italy, in the cost plans for public works, the (economic) space given to the category known as 'external works' is marginal, to the point of being almost optional: the first part of the budget that is sacrificed to lower bids.

But really, the shape and quality of public space is essential to civic life. Strolling in the shade of a tree-lined avenue, walking along a well-lit sidewalk in the evening, having a sit-down on a bench in a *piazza* or relaxing in a park, are al everyday events in the life of a city, that acquire value if experienced in spaces that are well-designed and well-built.

The pre-modern tradition of city-planning and landscaping was cocified in technical manuals giving the forms, typologies, vocabulary and architectural elements for outdoor spaces. Designing the void using stone or greenery, with trees, hedges, bushes, paving, fountains, street furniture, lamps and technical elements, required a skillful level of 'civic art'. Outdoor space was planned with the same attention and expertise invested in the design of a public building.

In the Italian Renaissance garden, the art of landscaping was as important as the other arts in the history of the world. Even in the city, vegetation was conceived as placing in contrast outdoor areas with a *natura naturans* character (think of the artificial wood at Villa Gamberaia) and those that were *natura naturata* (the rational artifice of the Italian garden). This was done through manuals of good practice and catalogues of solutions defining both architectural and landscape elements for the open spaces of the city. It was a genuine art. The physical consistency of open spaces in the city is historically of a dual nature: lithic and vegetal.

In recent years, the popularity of environmental awareness has led to renewed attention for the quality of public space, based on the notion that sustainability is found not only in ecological building, but also in the very nature of outdoor spaces. One of the most evident effects of this conviction is that designers have begun focusing hard on planting as being a solution with immediate mediagenic impact and easy to recognise.

This is a kind of 'green-worshipping' that increasingly comes across as an ephemeral ploy, rather than a solution, and a principle with which to address the question of long-term sustainability that is so essential in obtaining a more durable transformation of our built environment.

From: *Domus* n. 975 Dicembre / December 2013. Outdoor

5.6 Outdoor space: on landscape design

'Landscape architecture is probably the oldest and least recognised of all the physical arts [...] As people multiply and the surface of the land tends to be harnessed more and more to human needs, so it becomes paramount that the environment should be organised and made seemly [...] these studies are concerned with the artificial shaping of the land to accommodate the innumerable activities of the modern world [...] we have ahead of us, in the not too remote future, an art which could compare favourably with the great periods of the past.'[41]

There have been long periods - concurring with pre-modern times - in which people's days were shaped and regulated by slowness as we lived in harmony with the rhythms of nature. Instead the modern, contemporary era is marked by a continual flux of time and space that moves ever more quickly, subjected to continual mutation and acceleration. The transformation of the notion of outdoor space - public or private - is an emblematic example of this transformation.

The completeness of form found in the classical garden, in Ancient Greek and Roman times, up to the Renaissance garden based on the notion of *natura naturata*, bears clear and evident testimony to a principle that concerns both aesthetics and ethics with regard to classical man's place within the universe. Geometry, the human figure, movement and the environment were the elements of the world of ideas: the garden was the extension of the home into its surroundings and contained the same formal, material and artificial completeness. Outdoor space - when complete - was like a building, like a work of art: it pursued the same objectives of rest and stability but through rhythm, the differentiation, *'partitura'* and geometry of the elements were never inert and static. It defined true architecture in which the 'caprices' of nature were governed by the mind and rationality of man. The fundamental materials of the architecture of the classical garden were immutable, as

were those that defined architecture itself: stone, natural then, today increasingly artificial; mineral paths paved with gravel; evergreen vegetation modelled like geometry; water - meanwhile all the elements that changed with the seasons, like flowers and plants, were by definition unstable, they did not have a fixed place and were not part of the scheme of things: nature was the dispenser of materials but it was an intruder.

The contemporary house, like the classical villa, also extends into external areas; however, it takes quite a different approach. In today's terraces and gardens, space is defined by nature, it surrounds and creates the backdrop to real 'outdoor rooms', enclosed by green walls with the sky or a pergola acting as the ceiling. The style of these outdoor rooms is determined not so much by the form of the spaces as by the nature of the furniture, finishes and systems of lighting. Traditionally, winter gardens and conservatories have always been treated as 'glass rooms' connected to the house, that are decorated and furnished like an extra sitting-room. This approach is also evident in contemporary garden furniture, that conceals its special technical and functional characteristics, such as being weather-resistant or waterproof, to assume forms that are just like the furniture used indoors. A similar trend can be seen in floors, lighting and covering systems, in a recurring fusion – a cross-breeding – in which multiplicity and ubiquity appear to be the new categories when it comes to outdoor finishes and furniture.

Today we witness a phenomenon which in many ways shows opposite signs: in our frantic attempt to reconcile man and our pillaged, depleted environment, open spaces - whether public or private - are considered places where an overambitious, environment-friendly and ideological reconciliation takes place between man and nature. Thus 'urban gardens' appear wherever there are gaps and voids in the city, or on flat roofs , or on private terraces; roof gardens 'bloom' - euphemistically - also with vertical grass; facades are already green before they even begin tc be slowly covered by ivy or American vine; squares welcome trees, the city compensates the environment by replacing paving with lawns. Permaculture[42] promises new self-sufficiency for urban communities and imagines also adjusting to nature's cycle in the middle of the city. This is the eco-friendly myth of 'green idolatry', where open space, subjected to increasingly 'fast use' in the frantic pace of our modern times, seems to be destined to embrace the new utopia of a re-appropriation cf the man-made environment 'presided over' by nature.

From: *Domus* n. 986 Dicembre / December 2014. Outdoor

5.7 Outdoor space: on the need for 'the green element'

The green element and the house is the title of the 7th volume, edited by Luigi Figini in 1950, in *I Quaderni di Domus* series, edited by Lina Bo and Carlo Pagani.[43] It was a seemingly 'modest' publishing venture that managed to present effective solutions with regard to the transformation of the modern Italian home during the period following the Second World War. It succeeded in its intention, as indicated on the inside flap of the dust-jacket of the eleven volumes produced, 'through il-lustrated documentation and a technical approach to resolving the problem of fit-ting-out the modern home, according to efficient and scrupulously-chosen aesthetic criteria'. It is precisely this aim that explains the use of the 'singular' attributed to the term 'green element' in relation to man, the house, the city, new architecture.

Through case studies - an ordered catalogue of systems and technologies - Figini presents a selected review of practices and examples that seem to be based on a scientific model and in which the relationship between spaces and exterior elements - both artificial and natural - follows the idea of extending the space of the modern dwelling into 'concluded' external spaces: extensions to the home such as terraces, courtyards, private gardens and patios.

When addressing the question of designing outdoor spaces, it is usefu. to refer to this small book, which addresses invariant design strategies almost 70 years after its first publication. Its observations are still valuable and highly relevant. The text maintains that being attracted to greenery is a natural physiological condition for humans, along similar lines as basic life necessities such as eating and breathing - yet the urban habitat has gradually lost it. Transferring into spaces other than domestic ones has repressed and modified this natural instinct with confused in-terpretations of living, despite the fact that modernity has been working for a long time to put forward new forms and values for outdoor spaces, in the city and in the home. The excessive occupation of land that took place over the course of rampant urbanisation has in fact increased the value of outdoor spaces, particularly those residual to the house. Architecture should treat them with greater care and decorum, as with the most valuable and representative rooms of a building, and in the pre-modern eras of all civilisations, when great design was dedicated to green spaces and care given to their form.

Values were attributed to gardens, often through symbolic forms, linked to the sphere of leisure, rest, conviviality and contemplation. Mineral and plant elements were processed and transformed into a *natura naturata* that gave them the status of designed, built and inhabited 'architectural spaces'. Over the last fifteen years, a newfound awareness of the precious value of these spaces has been characterised by an array of elements of furniture and accessories for outdoor use. This explains the renewed sense of decor and richness that the world of high-end design and manufacturing has attributed to outdoor space, with diverse, original shapes and forms. The search for pleasure in outdoor living as an extension of the domestic setting has stimulated design responses for 'elements' that go beyond the 'old' role of being artificial accessories to decor, aspiring instead to provide solutions that are able to bestow autonomous formal qualities to spaces, like home furnishing.

The functional solutions offered are many and often ambiguous. Following the trends set by experiential marketing, these new products find in the rhetorical figure of synaesthesia one of the recurring ways to overcome market categories or fixed typologies: so plant-pots/lights or luminous sofas are now popular; blinds and mobile sunscreens are able not just to provide shade but to transform pergolas into covered spaces; sofas are covered in canopies to create a shell or an alcove; lamps imitate green hills or become sculptures; furniture like tables and chairs acquire a dignified status; tables are transformed into supports for plants and flowers; domestic flooring is extended outdoors and vice versa. This multiplicity of elements enables us to inhabit outdoor spaces more and more and to become, as well as citizens, also gardeners, cultivators, runners and city users. This new condition reaffirms a certain supremacy of practical activities that traditionally belong to the sphere of leisure over those that are more contemplative and speculative. Perhaps today there is no longer as much of a desire to think as there is a desire to do and do it preferably outdoors.

Nowadays, referring to the word 'element' in the singular, not to signify singularity but as an aesthetic model, responding in its variants to a unitary vocation of the modern, is no longer deemed valid. In fact, the condition of outmoded ideologies, multiple pressures and the individualised nature of our requirements, cannot be contained in the 'singular', but is fulfilled through an infinite range of solutions and spaces, also by cross-breeding the characters and vocations of elements in our human habitat.

We should therefore use the plural 'green elements' - where the reference to green can also be a mere allusion - to indicate not only the diversity, the richness of the solutions and products the market offers, but their transience and the speed of their consumption. With the green 'elements' we would like to redefine the outdoor category of the *Rassegna*, we are witnessing a phenomenon similar to the one which occurred with architecture and its aspiration to 'form', that today seems anachronistic before the succession of 'forms'. The 'equipment' that characterises our external spaces is increasingly blurred and indistinct compared to the products for our interior spaces. Differentiation is becoming less and less rigid. This contamination is recognisable in every category: in pergolas - that have the increasing tendency to enclose, as well as protect external spaces – but also in flooring, furniture, tables, sofas, lamps and finishes, that can just as much make our interiors feel like gardens as they can our exteriors feel like rooms. The living-room, combined with the aspiration for an extension of the home outdoors, continues to be a reference model in the design of systems and components for outdoors; these are charged with the specific demands of outdoor environments, defining not so much the formal and aesthetic characters of the products and components as much as their technical and functional requisites.

From: *Domus* n. 997 Dicembre / December 2015/ Domus n. 1007 Novembre / November 2016. Outdoor

Notes

37. Marco Zanuso, 'La Cucina/The Kitchen', in *Quaderni di Domus*, directed by Lina Bo and Carlo Pagani, Editoriale Domus, Milano 1945, p. 7.

38. C. Martino, 'LCD nell'industria della ceramica sanitaria', in *Green Report*, Catalano, 2013.

39. Jean Nouvel's description of his building for the CLM BBDO advertising agency in Paris. From a book edited by Giampiero Bosoni: *Jean Nouvel. Una lezione in Italia. Architettura e design 1976-1995*, p. 36.

40. Josef Stübben, *Der Städtebau*, Reprint of the first ed., 1890, Braunschweig und Wiesbaden, Vieweg & Sohn Verlag, 1980, p. 50.

41. Geoffrey Alan Jellicoe, *Studies in Landscape Design*, Oxford University Press, London, 1960

42. Bill Mollison; Reny Mia Slay, *Introduction to Permaculture*, 1991

43. Luigi Figini, 'L'elemento verde e l'abitazione', *Quaderni di Domus* n. 7, Collection curated by Franca Matricardi and Carlo Pagani, Milan 1950.

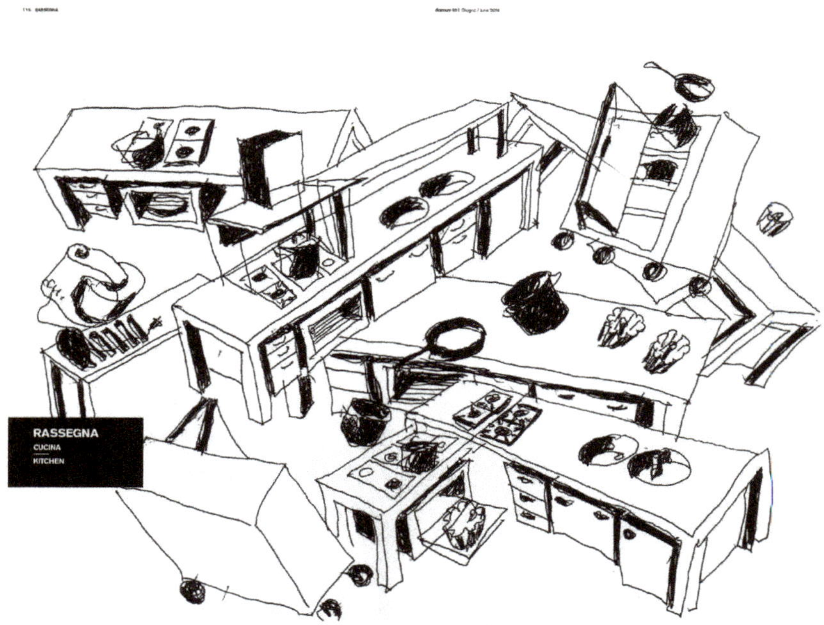

Figure 41.
Kitchens: innovation of forms, technologies and production.
Above: design sketch for the Banco kitchen, designed by Luca Meda for Dada, 1994;
Below: aluminium frames and panels; system New Logica, Valcucine, 2016

Figure 42.
Bathrooms: empathy and the evolution of production.
Above: A View of the Upper Parts of the Ruins of the Baths of Diocletian,
by Giovanni Battista Piranesi, etching with engraving, 1774.
Below: Thermal Baths in Vals, Design by Peter Zumthor, 1996

Figure 43.
Work spaces.
"Ink". A desk made of wood.
Design by Jasper Morrison for Molteni, Italy, 2016

Figure 44.
Work spaces.
Empathy and furniture design. Enhancing a culture of memory in daily life objects: the writing desk,
Eugenia Maria Canepone,
Supervisor: Spartaco Paris, Co-superviso : Sabrina Lucibello,
consultant: Antonacci Falegnamerie srl,
Master of Science in Product Design, Sapienza Univesità di Roma, 2017

Figure 45.
Work spaces.
La Passeggiate for WorkPlace 3.0,
Design by Michele De Lucchi for Salone del Mobile, Milano, 2015

Figure 46.
Outdoor space: open air spaces as public building.
Portico of the Roman Baths (Römischen Bäder) in the Sanssouci Park of Potsdam
by Karl Friedrich Schinkel, Germany, 1829-1840.

Figure 47.
Outdoor space: on landscape design.
Above: Charlottenhof Palace in the Sanssouci Park of Potsdam,
by Karl Friedrich Schinkel with Peter Joseph Lenné for the gardens, Germany, 1826-29.
Below: Family home, Dysart, Greystones, Ireland, Design Tome de Paor:
open air room among four concrete walls within a private garden and orchard, 2006

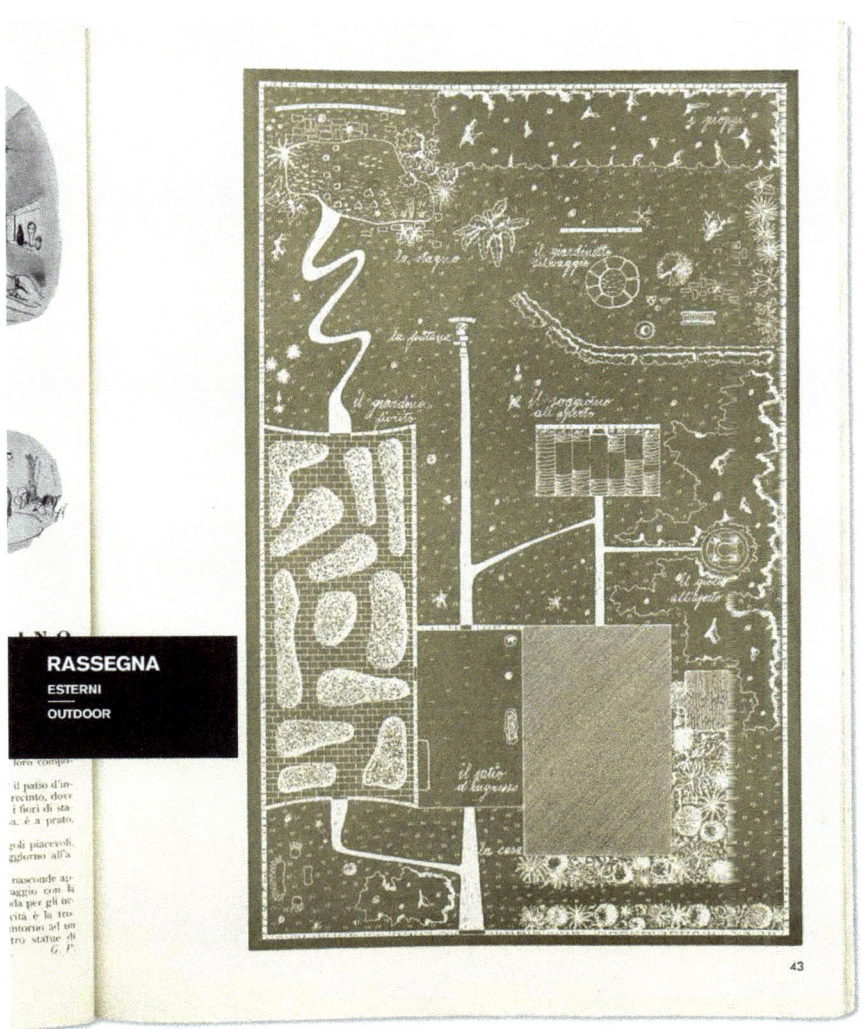

domus 987 Dicembre/ December 2015

Figure 48.
Outdoor space: on the need for 'the green element'.
Drawing of a garden design by Lina Bo Bardi and Carlo Pagani (from Domus 156, December 1940),
in Domus 997, December 2015
Image: Courtesy Editoriale Domus.

Figure 49.
The green element.
Model prototype, Hanging Gardens, 2016 Chongqing South Bank Residential-skyscraper Green Eco Space.
International Design Competition,
Design by Spartaco Paris, Roberto Bianchi

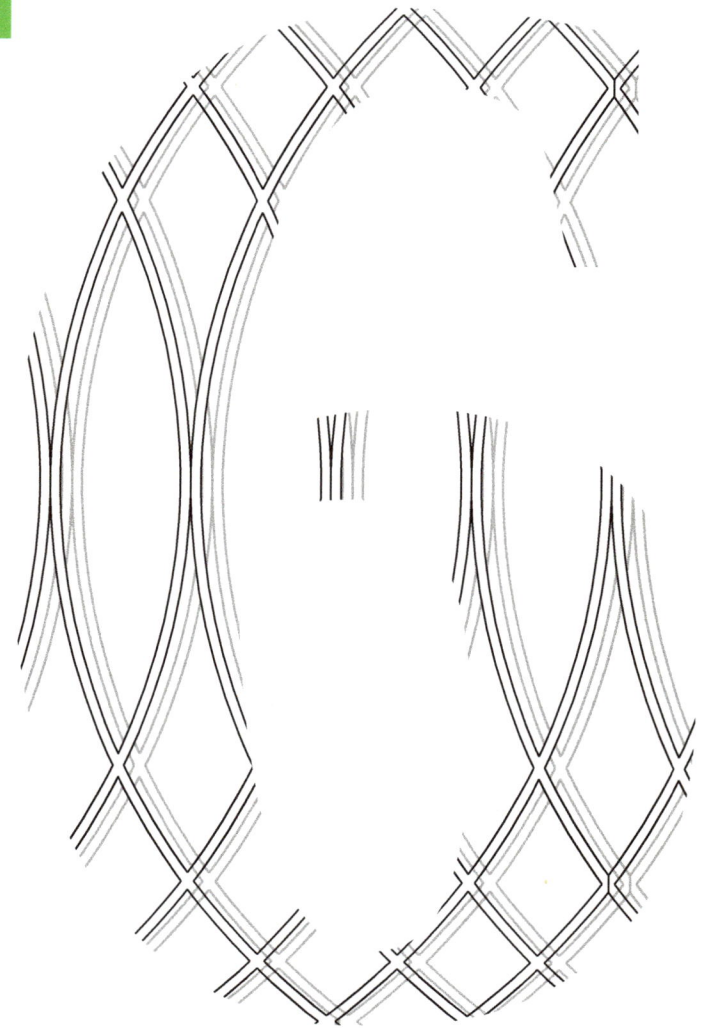

PART II
HOME
CHAPTER 6
TECHNOLOGIES FOR LIVING

6.1 Technological innovation and new forms in lighting design: the 2nd LED revolution

Every profound technological innovation brings about radical and, in some cases, revolutionary changes for designers who are confronted daily with the issue of what form objects should take. With mechanical, electronic or other technological advancements, there is always a transitional phase - whether it be long or short - in which innovations require time to be defined with an intrinsically corresponding form, in which the *Kernform and Kunstform* of the artifact correlate.

This lack of 'form' for new technologies is a recurring aspect in which there is a conflict between 'technological immanence' and 'cultural permanence' in the process of formal definition[44]. It is only when the specific formal immanence of a new technology has superseded the cultural permanence (stereotype) of the forms of a consolidated technique that a change, or leap, occurs in the invention, redefinition and diffusion of new forms.

This consideration can also be applied to the sphere of lighting design with the latest LED technology. The revolutionary scope and speed with which this new technology is evolving - with leading companies in the sector currently manufacturing around 40 per cent of their products using LED or OLED technologies - is still in a period of transition. The actual performance offered is in continuous development, to the point of rendering other consolidated technologies obsolete, and it is not yet possible to say that the process of formal definition offered by this technology is complete and stabilised.

As with other technological revolutions, the first effect on the form of devices is the proposal of consolidated forms derived from established technology. In the case of LED technology, the first evident aspect was a significant reduction in size for the same efficiency and performance compared to other technologies.

This reduction does not correspond to a fully-fledged exploration into the formal potential of LEDs, which instead still 'imitate' - with reduced dimensions - forms belonging to other technologies. Indeed, this development is entirely coherent with the transitional phase of a new technology. The reduction in technical thicknesses (in the order of just a few millimetres) of the LED light source, and above all its easy integration with digital systems, offer as yet unexplored possibilities, open to revolutionising the 'shape of light' in our offices and homes.

Leading manufacturers in the lighting sector are investing in innovative applications of LEDs primarily in the field of work and retail spaces, which represent the market sectors where demand and performance is most effective and measurable, and where the potential level of personalisation offered by LED technology can be reduced to a limited range of cases[45]. The time is not far off when in our domestic environments we will also be able to choose and alter artificial lighting conditions as desired, without having to change the fittings. Above all, however, it no longer seems like a far-off futuristic vision to herald the day in which artificial light will be emitted directly from the walls, ceilings and floors of our interiors.

The landscape of our domestic, work and urban surroundings is continually being enriched by the ever-increasing multitude of objects and designs that inhabit them. Among these, objects that emit and modulate artificial light are the elements that, in ever more complex and ambiguous forms and ways, contribute to arousing our emotions and stimulating our perception of space.

There are two distinct trends, quite different from one another but both closely linked to the opportunities presented by the development of new lighting technologies (LED and OLED). In the first case, fittings are not just restricted to being sources of light; their role has been extended further, particularly in the domestic sphere: the level of freedom they have acquired and the multiplicity of forms they have assumed have led them to become more and more like 'sculptures' for our homes. When it comes down to it, one of the characteristics of a well-designed product is that of being a beautiful object available to everyone (or almost) even when they substitute or surrogate the aspiration to possess and enjoy a work of art. As such, spaces are populated with light sculptures that are all different, but the result of mass-production, in many cases limited editions: they are simulacra of works of art in the age of technical reproduction. Furthermore, thanks to the opportunities offered by the miniaturisation of lighting objects and the integration of digital control systems, light itself assumes colours and effects that can be 'made to measure', with the aim of giving each of us the power to create our own lighting conditions.

The second horizon under exploration - also the consequence of technological innovation - is of a very different nature and concerns the possibility of disguising light sources as spatial elements, or incorporating them into items of furniture: this is the horizon where light is not just reflected off, but is directly emitted by walls, ceilings and furnishings.

In the end, both these scenarios tend to go beyond the poetic approach to the technical object, that which during the era of modern expansion regarded lighting as yet another 'place' of investigation and formal research, one in which the technical function has been able to influence forms and languages.

There are many striking inventions by great designers in the field of lighting that have found in technology - movement, orientation, modulation, switching, support, fixing - many places and pretexts for research and formal outcome

Think of the archetype of the table lamp: the Naska Loris by Jacobsen. A technical object endowed with its own formal expressiveness given by its technical elements - sprung movement, hinges, profiles, bases, clamps, buttons - it is the archetype of many table lamps that have found precisely in the formal exploration of connections and components, places for research and expression. Today we are seeing a miniaturisation of light sources along with the possibility of achieving similar if not better lighting conditions than the archetypes using much less energy: so the Naska

Loris becomes its ironic icon with the model Looksoflat by Stefan Geisbauer for Ingo Maurer; through its 'orthogonal projection', almost without thickness and immaterial - a 'surrealist' object amid thousands of lighting objects.

Domus n. 978 Marzo / March 2014. Domus n. 992 Giugno / June 2015 Lighting

6.2 Technological innovation and miniaturization in lighting design

Up until ten years ago, technical lighting elements in spaces could be reduced down to a number of families and categories, routinely present in manufacturers' catalogues: Fixed and directional spotlights, downlights, projectors, external fittings, hanging lamps, wall and ceiling-mounted lights, and a few others. Everything, however, depended on the dimensions of the lighting element: the incandescent, fluorescent or halogen bulb.

Even in the latter category one only has to consider the difference between the bulbs in the Naska Loris and the Tizio light; the luminarie and its conformation have always been conditioned by their size.

Nowadays, these conditions have undergone profound changes with the introduction of LED and OLED technology, used more and more and well-established in manufacturing.

Their energy efficiency is constantly increasing, while the energy they consume is getting less and less. From the point of view of the architecture of light, this technology, as well as making a decisive contribution to the miniaturisation of luminaries, enables the integration of computerised control systems. Each individual fitting can manage and modulate the desired lighting conditions, define colour temperature, greatly increase lighting intensity, reduce or eliminate annoying conditions such as glare. In fact, it is possible to determine optimal lighting conditions based on design requirements, working on the 'brain' of the light rather than the body. Evidence of this technological innovation can be seen in some recent successful designs for spaces and works of art where conservation issues impose complex and sophisticated performance requirements.

For example, thanks to LED technology, the new lighting system in the Sistine Chapel has resolved the need for reducing glare while maintaining a bright and uniform light on the ceiling frescoes - a technically-demanding undertaking– while remaining within the restrictions imposed by the need for protection and conservation. Another recent example is the new lighting for the Pietà by Rondanini, designed by Michele De Lucchi.

In this case, the design produced lighting conditions that are uniform, yet at the same time 'plastic' on the body of the statue, with impeccable control of the *chiaroscuro* effects. What is more, the light fittings do not interfere in the slightest with the space as they are positioned on the perimeter.

An interesting aspect of lighting technology design is, in fact, the control and management of light, whether it be computerised or inside the actual fittings and devices. It is a far cry from the old-fashioned on/off switches or even dimmers, that were the first devices to enable levels of lighting to be modulated. Digital technology, in a widespread and increasingly accessible way, enables the centralised and customised control of spaces, whether remotely or through digital detection systems. It is not a case of designing elements that, via their more or less integrated form, represent sources of light; instead there are opportunities to shape and configure spaces using light from increasingly intangible sources.

From: *Domus* n. 996 Novembre / November 2015. Lighting and home automation

6.3 The design of technological objects

If we look at the world of manufacturing, the area of product design for the home is continually extending its field of interest and application. The boundaries between art and craft are increasingly blurred, limited-edition productions are increasingly common and the hypothesis of greater product customisation seems to be more and more accessible. Research and development into products inherent to industrial culture therefore concern elements and components in which mass-production is a programmatic given. In the contemporary home this means a series of fixtures and finishes that, as a result of a demand for higher performance, necessitate that requisites be satisfied by industrial products that are extensively controlled, verified and certified. This process guarantees quality that can be verified in quantifiable terms, enabling demands to be met that concern human comfort and wellbeing (safety, ergonomics etc).

However, this does not always constitute aesthetic quality that is the real added value of products designed with talent and sensitivity. I refer to products that are seemingly anonymous in domestic interiors such as a switches, control panels, interior or exterior doors and handles. Together, these small details concur to define a comfortable, decorous and pleasant home environment.

At one time it was the skill of the craftsman and the quality of the materials, within shared formal rules, that determined and conferred quality onto a built artifact: well-executed casing or fluting, a planed edge, the profile of a window, the design of a floor or the moulding around a switch. Having said this though, it is true that even the most refined set of details does not make a space beautiful. Nowadays technology is a factor that can also determine style. Think of the BTicino switch from the Living Series designed by Giuseppe Zecca, Compasso d'Oro in 1989, in which for the first time colour was used as an element to give expressivity and grace to a technical object, or the anonymous but perfect cable-switch designed in 1968 by Achille and Pier Giacomo Castiglioni for VLM - exquisite examples of technical design in objects.

Today the trends regarding these aspects of interior design are heading towards two directions: heightening the tactile experience through research into materials and surfaces, as has been occurring now for some time with other technological products (such as all kinds of ICT devices) and at the same time a tendency to dissimulate materials and functions: this applies for example to the extensive range of flush or disappearing doors, that defy the classic archetypes, or surface finishes, where there is increasing ambiguity between the images evoked and the actual material; for doors and windows the use of multiple materials enables aesthetic demands to be combined with advanced technical performance. Worthy of note is the fact that these trends which emphasise fashions and styles - such as the bad simplification of minimalism - in some cases negate a series of pre-modern and classic principles that were the fruit of centuries-old knowledge and manufacture.

Only time will tell - and certainly not in our lifetime - whether many of these products are here to stay, becoming the new home classics, or will pass like seasonal fashions.

From: *Domus* n. 988 Febbraio / February 2015. Systems of Enclosure

Notes

44. Andrea Deplazes, 'Wood: indifferent, synthetic, abstract – plastic. Prefabrication technology in timber construction', in A. Deplazes (ed.), *Constructing Architecture. Materials, Processes Structures, a Handbook*, Birkhäuser, Basel 2005, p. 77.

45. A recent study carried out by the Nymphenburg Group for Zumtobel has made it possible to identify, in the field of technical illumination for shops, the emotional reactions of seven groups of clients to different recurring light scenarios according to a neuro-psychological model, in order to establish a specific range of lighting designs for each type of shops.

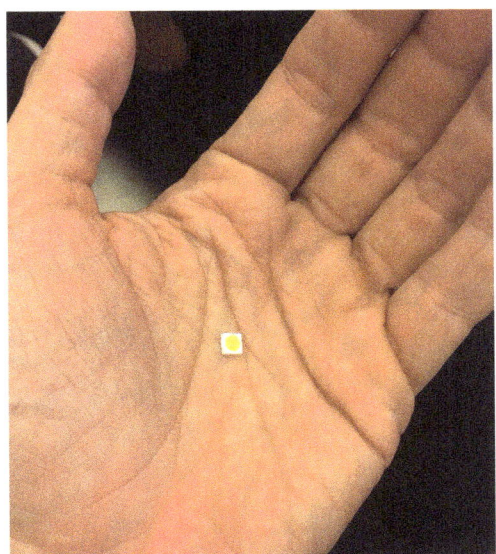

Figure 50.
Lighting and design of technological devices and equipment.
Above: Miniaturization;
Below: pc card as hardware of a LED system.

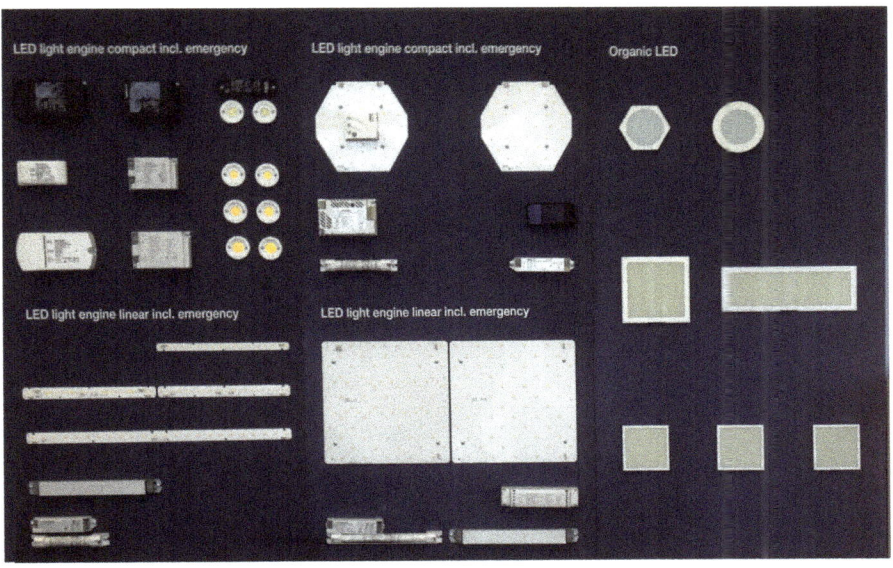

Figure 51a / 51b
Left page: TecLooksoflat, a desk-lamp designed by Stefan Geisbauer for Ingo Maurer in 2010
offers an ironic reworking of the model Naska Loris, designed in 1937 by Jac Jacobsen for Luxo.
Above: LED systems for emergency and Organic led, Tridonic, 2015.

Figure 52.
Technological innovation and new forms in lighting design.
Light&Light. Model prototype for home Led Light.
Master of Science in Product Design, Product Design Studio V,
prof. Spartaco Paris, prof. Sabrina Lucibello, in collaboration with Lumen Center.
Students: Safouan Azouzi, Stefano Silveri,
Sapienza, Università di Roma, 2017-2019

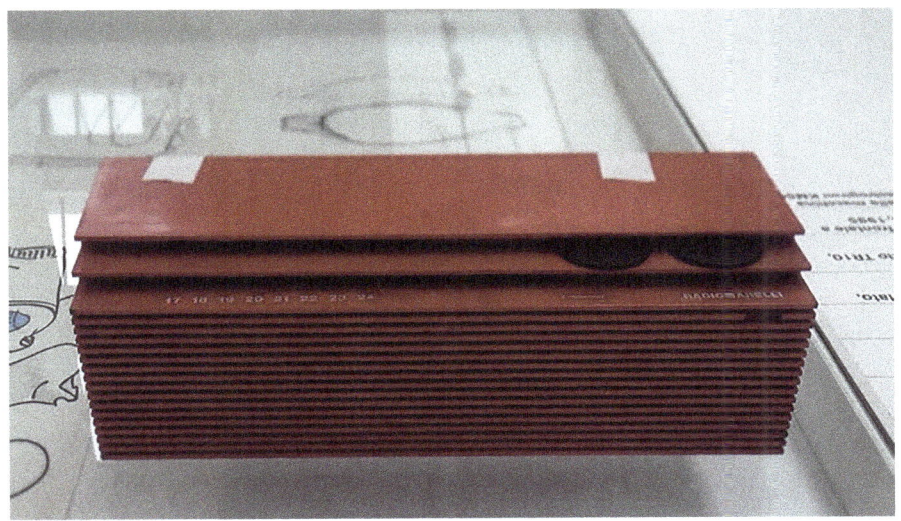

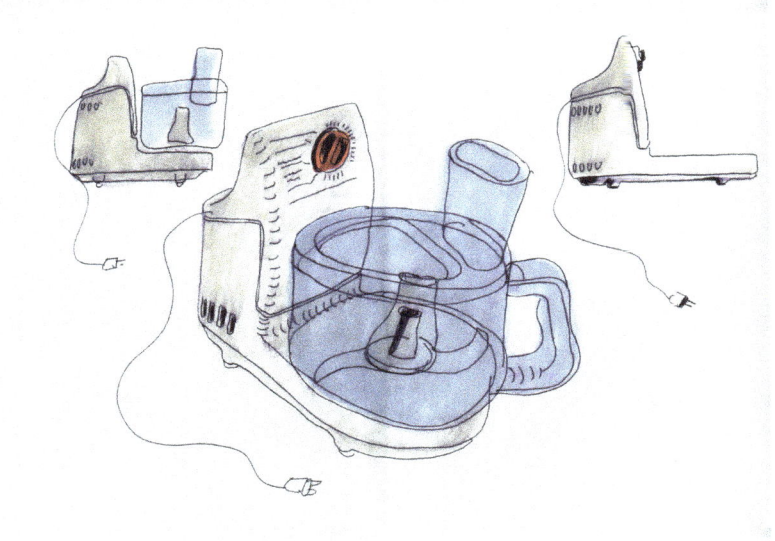

Figure 53.
The design of technological objects.
Above: radio device Radiomarelli B330, 1968, design by Luca Meda, at exhibit on Luca Meda.
La Felicità del progetto, Triennale di Milano, 2014;
Below: mixer, Girmi, KM31, 1984 design by Luca Meda,

Figure 54.
The phantasmagorical blackboard,
"Youthful Stories – Storie di Ventenn"' Exh bition Domus,
curated by Nicola Di Battista in collaboration with Domus Study Center,
Milano Fuorisalone Design week, 2015, Exhibit desig ı by Gianni Filindeu.

CREDITS

Introduction / Foreword

1. Cover of Rassegna n. 73 "Rivestimenti", Editrice Compositori, 1998, Bologna.

2. Courtesy of Editoriale Domus, Domus n. 979, April 2014, Domus 991 May 2015.

3. Courtesy of Editoriale Domus, Quaderni di Domus, 1945-1954.

4. Photo © Spartaco Paris.

5. a. Drawings: Courtesy of OFFICE Kersten Geers David Van Severen. b. Photo © Bas Princen.

6. Photo © Studio Ronan & Erwan Bouroullec.

7. Photo © from Judah, H. & Violette, R. (eds), Interwoven, Kvadrat textile and design. Munich. Prestel Verlag.

8. Photo ©Wikimedia Commons.

9. Cover of Wilhem Worringer, Abstraktion und Einfülung. Abstraction and Empathy. A contribution to the Psychology of style. 1908.

10. Courtesy of Kvadrat.

11. Courtesy of Editoriale Domus, Domus 990, April 2015.

12. Photo © Spartaco Paris.

13. Photo © Spartaco Paris.

1. Materials Sustainability In Design

14. Photo © Spartaco Paris.

15. Sapienza Università di Roma, Courtesy of Editoriale Domus, Domus 994, September 2015.

16. Courtesy of Editoriale Domus , Domus 983, September 2014.

17. Courtesy of Laminati Abet.

18. Sapienza Università di Roma.

19. Courtesy of Editoriale Domus, Domus 974, November 2013.

2. Envelopes/Surfaces/Facades

20. Photo © Spartaco Paris.

21. Photo © Spartaco Paris.

22. Photo © Spartaco Paris.

23. Photo © Spartaco Paris.

24. Photo © Spartaco Paris.

25. Photo © Spartaco Paris.

26. Photo © Spartaco Paris.

27. Photo © Spartaco Paris.

28. Drawing © Spartaco Paris, Roberto Bianchi.

3. Finishing

29. Photo © Spartaco Paris.

30. a. Photo © Spartaco Paris. b. Courtesy of 6a architects.

31. Photo © Droog.

32. Photo and drawings ©WOJR Organization for architecture.

33. Photo © Roos Alde Fotografie.

34. Josef Albers, M. Pierini (ed), J. Albers, Silvana Editoriale, Milan, 2011.

4. Furniture

35. Jan van Geest, Jean Prouvè Furniture, Benedikt Taschen Verlag GmBH 1991.

36. Courtesy of Cassina.it

37. Photo © Courtesy of Editoriale Domus, Domus 990 April, 2015.

38. Photo © Courtesy of Kevin Rice

39. Enzo Mari, Proposta per un'autoprogettazione, First Edition Centre Duchamp, 1974, Reprint by Corraini, 2002.

40. Ralph Caplan "The work of Charles and Ray Eames, ", UCLA Art Council / Frederick S. Wright Art Gallery; December 7, 1976-February 6, 1977

5. Types of Space

41. a. Università Iuav di Venezia- Archivio progetti Fondo Luca Meda, in Domus 981, Kitchens, 2015.
    b. Valcucine Catalogue, 2016.

42. a. View of the Upper Parts of the Ruins of the Baths of Diocletian, by Giovanni Battista Piranesi, etching with engraving, 1774.
    b. commons.wikimedia.org.

43. Photo © Courtesy of Molteni.

44. Photo © Courtesy of Eugenia Canepone, Sapienza Università di Roma.

45. Photo © Spartaco Paris.

46. Photo © Spartaco Paris.

47. a. Photo © Spartaco Paris.
    b. Photo © Courtesy of Tom de Paor.

48. Image: Courtesy of Editoriale Domus, Domus 997 April 2015.

49. Photo © Spartaco Paris.

6. Technologies for living

50. a. Photo © Spartaco Paris.
    b. Photo © Spartaco Paris.

51. a. Photo © Spartaco Paris.
    b. Photo © Spartacc Paris.

52. Sapienza Universita di Roma.

53. a. Photo © Spartacc Paris.
    b. Fondo Luca Meda, Archivio Progetti, Iuav.

54. a. Photo © Courtesy of Gianni Filindeu.

The texts by the author originally published in Domus between 2013 and 2017: Courtesy of Editoriale Domus.

REFERENCES

Albers, J. (2011). Teaching design. In: Marco Pierini (ed.), Josef Albers. Milano. Silvana Editoriale. Original text: Werklicher Formunterricht English translation by Frederick Amrine, Frederick Horowitz, and Nathan Horowitz Bauhaus, 2 no. 3, 1928

Aulenti, G. (1980). Una geometria mentale. In: Rassegna n. 4. Il disegno del mobile razionale in Italia 1928/1948. Bologna. Editrice Compositori.

Beccu M., & Paris S. (2008). Contemporary architectonic envelope between language and costruction [L'involucro architettonico contemporaneo tra linguaggio e costruzione]. Roma. RdesignPress.

Blaser, W. (1965) Mies van der Rohe: The Art of Structure. New York. Praeger.

Boeri, C., & Pagani, C. (eds.) (1952). Le tende nella casa. Serie Quaderni di Domus, n. 10. Milano. Editoriale Domus.

Borachia, V., & Pagani, C. (eds.) (1950). Sedie, divani, poltrone. Serie Quaderni di Domus. n. 8. Milano. Editoriale Domus.

Borachia, V., & Pagani, C. (eds.) (1951). I letti. Serie Quaderni di Domus. n. 9. Milano. Editoriale Domus.

Borachia, V., & Pagani, C. (eds.) (1954). I soggiorni. Serie Quaderni di Domus. n. 9. Milano. Editoriale Domus.

Bosoni, G. (1996). Jean Nouvel. Una lezione in Italia. Architettura e design 1976-1995. Milano. Skira

Bruno, G. (2002). Atlas of emotion: Journeys in Art, Architecture, Film. New York. Verso.

Bruno, G. (2014). Surface: Matters of Aesthetics, Materiality and Media, Chicago. University of Chicago Press.

Calvino, I. (1981). Italiani vi esorto ai classici. In: L'Espresso, 20 June 1981. Roma. Gruppo Editoriale Espresso.

Calvino, I. (1988). Six Memos for the Next Millennium. Cambridge. Massachusetts. Harvard University Press.

Canella L., & Radici, R. (eds) (1948). Tavoli e piani d'appoggio. Serie Quaderni di Domus, n. 6. Milano. Editoriale Domus.

Caplan, R., (1977). Making Connections: The Work of Charles and Ray Eames. In: Connections: The Work of Charles and Ray Eames. Los Angeles. University of California.

Carullo R., & Pagliarulo R. (2013). Actions on surfaces. Softness. Soveria Mannelli (Catanzaro). Rubbettino.

Collina L., & Zucchi C. (eds.) (2016). Sempering. Process and pattern in architecture and design. Milano. Silvana Editoriale.

Damiani, L. (2014). Questioni di Design/Design matters. In: Domus n. 980, maggio/May 2014. Milano. Editoriale Domus.

De Fusco, R. (2007). Storia del design. Roma-Bari. Laterza.

Del Curto, B., Fiorani, E., Passaro, C. (2010). La pelle del Design. Progettare la sensorialità. Milano. Lupetti.

Deplazes, A. (ed.) (2005). Constructing Architecture. Materials, Processes, Structures, a Handbook, Basel. Birkhäuser Publisher.

Donghi, D. (1923). Manuale dell'architetto. Torino. Utet.

Dubois, M., (1998). La dimensione del tavolo. The table dimension. In: Lotus International n. 98. Costruzioni. Tectonics. Milano. Editoriale Lotus.

Figini, L. (ed.) (1950). L'elemento verde e l'abitazione. Serie Quaderni di Domus, n. 7. Milano. Editoriale Domus.

Franzen, J. (2011). Liking Is for Cowards. Go for What Hurts. Commencement Speech, Kenyon College, May 21, 2011. In: New York Times, May 28, 2011. New York.

Frampton, K. (1985). Mies van der Rohe: Avant-Garde and Continuity. In: Studies in Tectonic Culture. Houston. Rice University.

Fuller, B. (2011). La pelle dell'edificio storico. Valori patrimoniali e tecnici della prassi del restauro dell'involucro. In: Riuso del patrimonio architettonico, Bruno Reichlin and Bruno Pedretti (eds.), Mendrisio. Silvana Editoriale.

Galimberti, U. (2000). Psiche e techne. L'uomo nell'età della tecnica. Milano. Feltrinelli.

Gandolfi, V. (ed.) (1945). Gli studi nella casa. Serie Quaderni di Domus, n. 3. Milano. Editoriale Domus.

Gregotti, V. (1998). Editoriale. In: Rassegna, Ri-vestimenti, n. 73. Bologna. Editrice Compositori

Grignolo, R. (ed.) (2013). Marco Zanuso. Scritti sulle tecniche di produzione e di progetto. Mendrisio. Silvana Editoriale.

Huber, B., & Steinegger, J.C. (eds.) (1971). Jean Prouvé. Une architecture par l'industrie. Architektur aus der Fabrik. Industrial Architecture. Zürich. Les Éditions d'Architecture Artemis

Itten, J. (1974). The Art of Color. New York. John Wiley and Sons Original title: Kunst der Farbe, Ravensburg. 1961.

Jellicoe, G.A. (1960). Studies in Landscape Design. London. Oxford University Press.

Jongerius, H. (2015). Start by designing the yarn. [Il progetto parte sempre da un filo]. Domus. La città dell'uomo, n. 990. Milano. Editoriale Domus.

Kleinman, K., & Leslie Van Duzer, L. (2005). Mies van der Rohe. The Krefeld Villas. New York . Princeton, Architectural Press.

Ladis, V. (ed.) (1945). I libri nella casa. Serie Quaderni di Domus. n. 1. Milano. Editoriale Domus.

Latouche, S. (2007). Petit traité de la décroissance sereine. 1001 Nuits. Paris. France.

Magnago Lampugnani, V. (2016) Five Proposals for Building in Uncertain Times. In: Domus, n.1000, Milano. Editoriale Domus.

Maldonado T., & Obrist H.U. (2010). Arte e Artefatti. Milano Feltrinelli.

Mari, E. (2002) Proposta per un'autoprogettazione, First Edition Centre Duchamp, 1974, Reprint ed by Corraini, 2002.

Mollison, B, & Slay M.R. (1991). Introduction to Permaculture. Tasmania. Australia. Tagari Publications.

Munari, B. (2005). Introduzione. In: Albers, J. Interazione del colore. Esercizi per imparare a vedere. Milano. Il Saggiatore, pp. 8-9.

Olivieri, L.C. (ed.) (1946). L'illuminazione della casa. Serie Quaderni di Domus, n. 5. Milano. Editoriale Domus.

Paris, S. (2013), Design and technology. Lectures. Trento, List Publisher.

Paris, S. (2013). A Table is like a Building. Archetipo di architettura. In: "A design selection". Diid Disegno Industriale | Industrial Design n. 56. Rome. RDesign press.

Paris, S. (ed.) (2015). Green Materials. Domus Green. La città dell'uomo, n. 994. Milano. Editoriale Domus.

Paris, S. (2017). Jean Prouvé e l'esperienza dell'architettura come prodotto industriale'. In: M. Perriccioli (ed.). Pensiero tecnico e cultura del progetto. Riflessioni sulla ricerca tecnologica in architettura. Milano. Franco Angeli.

Peach, S., & Judah H.. (2013). The resurrection of fabric in architecture. In: Judah, H. & Violette, R. (eds.), Interwoven, Kvadrat textile and design. Munich. Prestel Verlag.

Persico, E. (1930). Tendenze e realizzazioni. In: 'La casa bella' n. 29, May. Milano.

Picchi F. (1998). Prouvé inventore: 32 Brevetti. Prouvé, the inventor. 32 Patents. In: Domus 807. Milano. Editoriale Domus. pp. 52-66.

Rykwert, J. (1988). L'architettura è tutta nella superficie. Semper e il principio del rivestimento. Architecture lies in the surface. Semper and the cladding principle. In: Rassegna, Ri-vestimenti, n. 73. Bologna. Editrice Compositori.

Rykwert, J. (1990). Morfologia di Semper. In: Rassegna, ' I sensi del decoro, n.41'. Bologna. Editrice Compositori.

Schmitt, B.H. (1999). Experiential Marketing: How to Get Customers to Sense, Feel, Think, Act, Relate to Your Company and Brands. London. Simon and Schuster.

Stübben, J. (1980). Der Städtebau. Reprint of the first ed., 1890, Braunschweig und Wiesbaden, Vieweg & Sohn Verlag.

Tafuri M. (1976). Architecture and Utopia. Cambridge. Massachusetts. The MIT Press.

Tevarotto, M. (ed.) (1945). Camini. Serie Quaderni di Domus, n. 4. Milano. Editoriale Domus.

Ursprung P. (2005). Herzog & de Meuron: natural history. Baden. Lars Müller Publishers.

Van Geest, J. (1991). Jean Prouve Furniture. Bonn. Benedikt Taschen Verlag.

Vitta, M. (2008). Dell'abitare. Corpi spazi oggetti immagini. Milano. Einaudi.

Worringer, W. (1997). Abstraction and Empathy. A Contribution to the Psychology of Style. Chicago. Elephant Paperbacks. Original Title: Abstraktion und Einfüldung. Ein Betrag zur Stilpsychologie. 1908. R. Piper Verlag. München.

Zanuso M. (ed.) (1945). La Cucina. Serie Quaderni di Domus, n. 4 Milano. Editoriale Domus.

Zaera-Polo, A. , Trüby, S., AMO, Harvard Graduate School of Design, Koolhaas, R., Boom, I. (2014).

Zhang, L. (ed.) (2018). Junya Ishigmami. Freeing Architecture. Fondation Cartier pour l'art contemporain. Tokyo, LIXIL Publishing.

CPSIA information can be obtained
at www.ICGtesting.com
Printed in the USA
BVHW022017280719
554531BV00011B/466/P